Real Life Cooking

Trish Deseine

Real Life Cooking

Photography by Sylvain Thomas

HACHETTE
Illustrated

Simmer, stew, infuse, caramelize, preserve ... All these
words evoke the delicious food of our childhood, those
dishes our mothers and grandmothers sprinkled with
generous pinches of love.

However, our lives have changed. Hemmed in by constraints and
commitments, our schedules are becoming more and more hectic.
How can we possibly cook like our mothers and grandmothers did?
And yet...

Time is one of the essential ingredients of these recipes. They fit in
perfectly with modern-day life and help us rediscover food we used to
know and love. They can be made when we want and are adapted to
our way of life, not the other way round!

This is because these dishes, which are made with the best ingredients,
can easily be reheated, left on the stove or in the oven, or kept in the
refrigerator overnight. Their flavor will simply improve as you go about
your everyday business.

Real Life Cooking contains a collection of well-known and not so
well-known recipes inspired by French, Mediterranean, British,
American, and Asian cuisine. By following these revised and simplified
versions, even beginners, used to the limitations of their local stores,
can succeed.

Nuts

This book includes dishes made with nuts and nut derivatives. It is advisable for readers with known
allergic reactions to nuts and nut derivatives and those who may be potentially vulnerable to these
allergies, such as pregnant and nursing mothers, invalids, the elderly, babies and children, to avoid
dishes made with nuts and nut oils. It is also prudent to check the labels of pre-prepared ingredients
for the possible inclusion of nut derivatives.

APPETIZERS

In my house, blinis with taramasalata are off the menu. When I used to make them in advance, I dished them up in all their cold, gelatinous splendor, bright red round the edges and all shriveled up. When my desire to serve fresh blinis saw me putting all four slots of my toaster to use, I spent my whole time rushing between the kitchen and the living room, missing all the evening's juiciest gossip as I did so. My guests sat down to eat tipsy and famished, discouraged from claiming more than two blinis each by the hint of menace in their hostess's voice as she asked, "I don't suppose anybody wants another blini?"

My catchphrase now is "back to basics." I've started having fascinating philosophical discussions with my pork butcher and cheese specialist on the origins and technical aspects of ripening cheese and other delicacies. I choose my appetizers; I don't make them any more.

I cut cheese into pretty little pieces and serve it with broiled pine nuts, macadamias or Brazil nuts (even prepared in advance, they behave impeccably) and tapas-style quince jelly (membrillo), if I manage to unearth some. In summer, I serve buffalo milk mozzarella (readily available these days), feta cheese, or little fresh goats' cheeses marinated in herbs.
If I'm serving ham, I cut it into tiny little slices.
Don't forget the raw vegetables for those who don't want to eat too much before the meal or who appreciate a variety of colors (cherry tomatoes, carrots, stalks of cucumber), chilled fruit (melon, watermelon, figs, apricots in season), a little bread with some *fleur de sel* (page 18) sea salt and—why not?—some good quality olive oil.

And don't forget:

"If you serve a plate of hearty appetizers, you can dispense with boring old first courses."

Tête de moine with roast tomatoes

A friend discovered this. Tête de moine (monk's head) is a cows' milk cheese with a soft sticky rind, from Switzerland. Although no other cheese melts in the mouth quite like a Tête de moine you can replace it with Edam or a young mimolette—but don't forget to remove the rind!

Serves as many as you like
Preparation time: 5 minutes
Cooking time: 2 hours

1 ovenproof dish
1 girolle or circular cheese grater (illustrated)
1 Tête de moine cheese (or Edam or a young mimolette)
3 or 4 bunches of cherry tomatoes
olive oil
salt, pepper
chunks of farmhouse bread

Preheat the oven to 250° F.

Put the tomatoes in an ovenproof dish and drizzle a little olive oil over them. Shake the dish to distribute the oil so the tomatoes do not stick.

Roast for about 2 hours.

Serve the tomatoes with the cheese, mounted on the girolle, some interesting bread, salt, and pepper and let everyone help themselves.

Like all the other recipes in this book, these ones need time if they are to be enjoyed at their best. They can just sit peacefully in your kitchen cupboards, cellar, or refrigerator. Some will improve in flavor as a result and you'll always have something delicious and easy to offer your guests, even unexpected ones.

Camembert baked in its box

Serves 6
Preparation time: 30 seconds
Cooking time: 15–20 minutes

2 good Camemberts
raw vegetables and fruit cut into sticks
some thick, crusty bread

Preheat the oven to 350° F.
Take the paper wrappers off the Camemberts; put the cheeses back in their boxes and bake them in the oven for 15 to 20 minutes until they are completely liquefied.
Lift off the lids, split open the crust from the top and serve as a dip with raw vegetables, apples, apple slices, chicory leaves, celery stalks, and some good, crusty bread.

Mature cheeses

Serving some good cheese with an aperitif is an excellent way of doing without a first course while at the same time discovering the best products from the French regions and across the entire world.
Our taste buds are keenest before a meal, and serving some mouth-watering cheeses can quickly turn into a convivial occasion for sampling new delicacies, particularly if they are accompanied by wines from the same region or ones that combine perfectly with the cheeses.
But be careful. I said convivial! Don't turn the occasion into a lecture. The details of your research and your choices are as interesting to you as they are boring to your guests.
Here are some suggestions for interesting taste combinations:

Roquefort/dried pears
Stilton/apricots
Mimolette/apples
Parmesan/broiled pine nuts
Manchego/quince jelly (membrillo)
Cheddar/chutney
Tomme cheese/black-cherry jam

Fresh and marinated cheeses

These cheeses (feta, mozzarella, fresh goats' cheeses, ricotta) require a little more equipment: small plates, cutlery and napkins are essential. In summer, accompanied by a well chilled rosé, they are an excellent way of killing time while the chops chargrill on the barbecue (page 184).
All these cheeses will keep well in a cool place, marinated in olive oil enlivened with herbs, lemon juice, garlic, chili, or simply salt and pepper.

Apple slices with lime

Serves 6
Preparation time: 15 minutes
Cooking time: 1½ hours

1 baking sheet lined with greaseproof paper or 1 silicone baking sheet
1 wire rack

1 cup sugar
juice and grated rind of 1 lime
2 crisp green apples

Preheat the oven to 225° F.
Put the sugar in a pan with the lime juice and rind. Heat until the sugar has melted. Boil the syrup over gentle heat for 5 minutes.
Slice the apples very finely. Put the slices into the syrup for 3 minutes. Remove with a slotted spoon, place on the baking sheet and bake in the oven for 1½ hours.
Leave to cool on a wire rack.

Raw ham

I first saw raw ham served with melon when I was 18, and I thought the lady of the house had forgotten to cook it. Last week, I still thought that Aosta ham came from Italy. For these two reasons, I have nothing to contribute on the subject of ham.

Let me just say that the years of experience and love invested in the making of a good ham will always be reflected in the taste. So buy the best. But you knew that already, didn't you?

Fresh and canned sardines

Fresh sardines are relatively easy to clean and fillet, but the fish seller's assistance is invaluable...

Marinate them in olive oil with herbs and lemon juice then put them on slices of toast, adding a sundried tomato if you happen to have some.

Take advantage of the fashion for sardines millésimées ("vintage sardines") to serve the trendiest appetizer around at the moment. To attain the height of sophisticated simplicity, lay your sardine lovingly on a bed of butter salted with fleur de sel from the salterns of the village of Portes en Ré (see below) or just leave it lying nonchalantly in its luxury can.

If you've retained your common sense and have only a can of ordinary sardines, mix your humble fish with some good cream cheese, lemon juice and a little chili powder before spreading them on toast.

Raw, sundried, and roast tomatoes

It's crazy, but this morning I found 6 varieties of tomatoes at my grocery store. Fortunately, taste is now one of the considerations in the rush to create ever more varieties: the cherry tomatoes you serve with your apéritifs—with *fleur de sel* of course, and olive oil—might even be good.

Sundried tomatoes in a jar or bought loose will fit the bill nicely. They have the advantage of being marinated in advance.

If you really want to spoil your guests, take the time to roast some tomatoes (page 138). All you need to do then is to put them on some slices of toast, possibly rubbed with garlic, and then sit back and await the flood of compliments.

Marinated, broiled bell peppers

I think these are just wonderful. They're a bit tedious to prepare, but they're better homemade than bought in a jar (page 136).

Cidre des Glaces

An apple wine made from late harvested apples. Absolutely delicious with mature Mimolette or cheddar.

Ice wine

A luxury wine made from late harvested grapes that makes a splendid accompaniment for foie gras or blue cheese.

Fleur de sel

Another cult product, this sea salt is harvested by traditional methods in the coastal area of Guérande, Brittany. It'll stay in fashion longer than pedigree sardines, I'll warrant you.

It has supplanted ordinary salt and given rise to all sorts of products: lightly salted butter with fleur de sel, rillettes with fleur de sel, chips with fleur de sel, and so on.

How long will it be before we get premium fleur de sel?

Personal message to Catherine M: there's no point putting it in the water you cook your pasta in.

FAMILY WEEKENDS

Just because we don't have any time to spare, it doesn't mean we have to do everything at top speed. Let me explain . . .

For some time, sociologists have been telling us repeatedly that we are all longing to get back to the fundamental things of life and to enjoy ourselves again. Instead, the pace of life just goes on increasing remorselessly around us.

When it comes to food, we are bombarded with ideas for dishes that can be created in minutes. But in the end, if your weekends are anything like mine, you will realize that it's better to have food available when you want it than to let your schedule be dictated by the recipes you've chosen.

It's so much easier to cook for an hour or two when it suits you and to leave everything to simmer, infuse, marinate, or simply cool until you want to sit down to eat.

For me, the most enjoyable times at the weekend are the ones that are least expected: an invitation for the evening sent out the morning before, or a cup of tea that goes on until dinner time... These healthy, nourishing dishes, which can be prepared as and when you wish, will delight everyone who eats with you, at whatever time of day.

THANKS TO THE LADY IN THE PHOTO FOR GIVING ME THIS RICH, TASTY RECIPE. She has very firm views on the cooking liquid: for her, diluting the wine with water is absolutely out of the question. If the amount of liquid falls to a critical level, you simply have to open another bottle!

Market stallholders are one of my main sources of inspiration. In the beginning, they all took me for a slightly crazy tourist. Now I think they're proud to share their knowledge and expertise. Sometimes a simple question can trigger off a lively discussion, with half the people in the market joining in.

Beef in wine

Serves 6–8
Preparation time: 20 minutes
Cooking time: 3 hours

1 large casserole dish

2 tablespoons olive oil
3 lb 5 oz braising steak
3 carrots, peeled and cut into rounds
3 turnips, peeled and chopped
2 stalks celery, chopped
thyme, bay leaves
1 bottle wine (at least!)
1 onion, stuck with 2 cloves
salt and pepper

Heat the oil in the casserole dish and brown the meat all over.

Add the vegetables and herbs and continue to cook for a few minutes. Pour in the wine, add the onion and a little salt and pepper, but not too much because the liquid will reduce a lot.

Cover and cook over gentle heat for at least 3 hours. If the cooking liquid reduces too much; don't even think of diluting it with water—open another bottle!

Variations

Substitute pork shoulder for the beef and hard cider for the wine. You could even add a few peeled apples to the casserole 20 minutes before the end of the cooking time.

A brief anatomy lesson

Beef
Cuts for braising or stewing
Neck
Chuck
Shank
Fore rib
Tail
Brisket
Flank
Skirt
Round
Chuck steak

Veal
Cuts for braising or stewing
Blade
Hock
Flank
Shank
Breast
Shoulder
Neck
Middle ribs

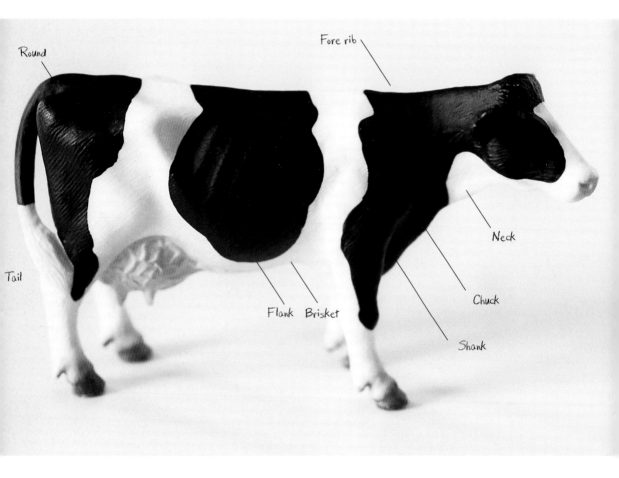

Lamb

Cuts for braising or stewing

Shoulder
Shank
Breast
Neck

For slow roasting

Leg
Shoulder

Pork

Cuts for braising or stewing

Hock
Pig's feet
Knuckle
Belly
Ribs
Shoulder

For slow roasting

Belly
Shoulder
Loin
Leg

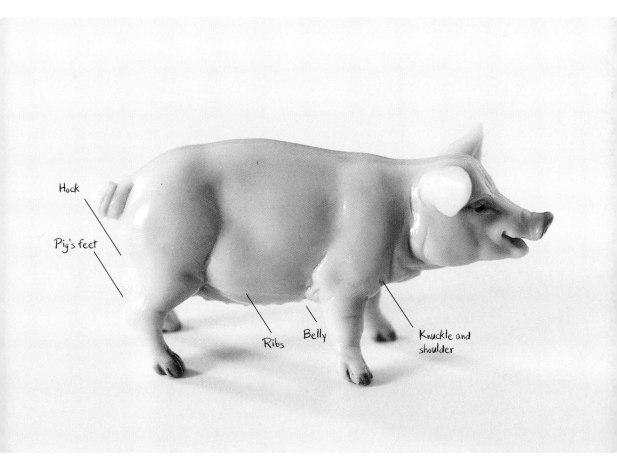

Hock

Pig's feet

Ribs

Belly

Knuckle and shoulder

MAYBE IT'S BECAUSE I HAVEN'T LIVED LONG ENOUGH IN FRANCE, but I avoid any identifiable part of an animal's body like the plague. I still don't know how anyone can cook a calf's foot, a sheep's brain, or a pig's ear or snout.

Ox or calf's tail and cheek have one major advantage. Although in France they're classed as cheap cuts and are displayed on the tripe butcher's stand along with the offal, or variety meats, that I find a little yuk, they're absolutely delicious. When it comes down to it, they look just like cutlets, albeit very round ones, and taste like skirt of beef.

Even so, you still have to trust your butcher implicitly. For me, that's no problem at all. We get along just fine. What's more, I have the dubious privilege of saying hello every morning to my future stews and casseroles as they graze in a field right next to my house. They answer my greeting with a nonchalant swish of the main ingredient in this recipe…

Beef stew with carrots

A long way from the current craze for world food, this classic is as easy to prepare as it is pleasing to (re)discover.

Serves 6–8
Preparation time: 25 minutes
Cooking time: 3 hours

1 large casserole dish

2 tablespoons olive oil
3 lb 5 oz beef (shoulder or chuck steak)
3 lb 5 oz carrots, cut into rounds
4 onions, chopped
thyme, bay leaves
1¼ cups white wine
salt and pepper

Heat the oil in the casserole dish and brown the meat all over. Add the vegetables and herbs and cook for several minutes. Pour in the wine and enough water to half cover the meat. Season with salt and pepper (but don't overdo it, because the cooking liquid will reduce a lot), bring to a boil and leave to simmer over gentle heat for 3 hours.

Oxtail stew

Serves 6–8
Preparation time: 20 minutes
Cooking time: 2½–3 hours

1 large casserole dish

3 leeks
3 carrots
2 turnips
1 stalk celery
1 onion, stuck with 4 cloves
thyme, bay leaves, and parsley
1¼ cups white wine
salt and pepper
2 lb 4 oz oxtail, sliced and tied together with string (as illustrated)
To serve
sea salt
mustard

Peel and roughly chop the vegetables and place them in the casserole dish with the wine, herbs and some salt and pepper (but not too much because the cooking liquid will reduce considerably). Add enough water to cover the vegetables, bring to a boil, and add the meat. Simmer over a low flame for 2½ to 3 hours, skimming off excess fat from time to time. Season the stock, strain, and serve separately if you wish (for example, with floating pasta you have cooked in it—see page 120).
Serve the meat surrounded by vegetables with the sea salt and mustard.

Pork in white wine

Serves 6
Preparation time: 10 minutes
Cooking time: 2–3 hours

1 large pan

1 knuckle of pork
2 carrots, cut into rounds
1 onion stuck with 2 cloves
1 stalk celery, chopped
1 bouquet garni
5 black peppercorns
rind of 1 orange
2 cups white wine
salt

Place all the ingredients in a large pan, bring to a boil, skim off excess fat, and simmer for 2 to 3 hours.
Serve hot with apple compote, mashed potatoes, peas, and Cumberland sauce.

Cumberland sauce

Preparation time: 5 minutes
Cooking time: 10 minutes
Cooling time: 2 hours

1 pan

2 oranges
2 lemons
2 shallots, finely chopped
1 tablespoon mustard
½ cup redcurrant jelly
½ cup port
2 teaspoons cornstarch

Grate the rind of 1 orange and 1 lemon. Squeeze the juice from all the fruit. Put it in a pan with the shallots, the mustard, and the redcurrant jelly. Cook for 5 minutes then add the port. Dissolve the cornflour in a tablespoon of water and add it to the sauce. Cook for a few minutes, stirring constantly, then add the orange and lemon rind and leave to cool before serving.

Roast belly of pork in honey

A dish as rich in taste as it is in calories. Even though much of the fat gets lost in the cooking, it's better to serve it without a first course and to round off the meal with a particularly light dessert.

Serves 6
Preparation time: 10 minutes
Cooking time: 3 hours

1 roasting pan

3 lb 5 oz belly of pork
salt and pepper
3 or 4 cloves (optional)
1 tablespoon olive oil
3 tablespoons honey

Preheat the oven to 350° F.
Ask your butcher to score the rind as in the photo. Otherwise, take a sharp knife and do it yourself.
Rub the rind with salt and pepper, pressing the seasoning into the incisions. Stick the cloves into the rind. Then pour the olive oil over the meat. Put the meat in the oven and leave to cook for 1 hour, basting it from time to time.
After a further 1½ hours—you will have basted it two or three times by now—take the meat out of the oven, increase the temperature and spread the honey over the pork rind. Cook for another 30 minutes, basting it twice more.
Take the meat out of the oven and leave to stand for 10 minutes. Season and serve accompanied by a purée of peas with pieces of chopped bacon (page 144).

Turn the oven down!

It's strange, but what we all want nowadays is meat cooked slowly in the oven until it is almost caramelized, very tender and soft. How is it done? Well, before cooking it, rub your piece of meat with oil and herbs or spices, then heat your oven to a low temperature and take your time. The kinds of meat that lend themselves best to this treatment are pork (belly, shoulder or leg end) and lamb (leg or shoulder). As soon as you feel at home with this general method of cooking, you can start to vary the herbs, vegetables, wines, and spices listed in these recipes and create your own variations.

Roast leg of lamb

As amenable as a lamb gamboling meekly in its meadow, a leg of lamb can just as easily be cooked fast at a high temperature, or slowly at a lower temperature.

Serves 8–10
Preparation time: 5 minutes
Cooking time: approximately 4 hours

1 roasting pan with a rack
1 mini food processor

1 leg lamb about 3 lb 5 oz–4 lb 8 oz in weight
4–5 tablespoons olive oil
4 cloves garlic, crushed
salt and pepper
thyme and rosemary, chopped very finely

Preheat the oven to 250° F.
Take the meat out of the refrigerator at least 30 minutes before putting it in the oven.
Blend the other ingredients together to make a paste and rub well into the meat, making sure you cover the entire surface. You can also stick some garlic into the meat by making little incisions here and there. Roast the meat for about 4 hours, longer if it is a large joint, basting it as often as possible.
Take the opportunity to enjoy the delicious aroma that will fill your kitchen.
Serve with roast vegetables, ratatouille, or tians (pages 136–42).

Leg of lamb braised with vegetables

This method is similar to that used to make the Alsatian specialty baeckeoffe and leaves the meat tender and full of flavor. A traditional baeckeoffe dish is a large clay terrine but a large heavy casserole dish or slow cooker will serve the same purpose.

Preparation time: 20 minutes
Cooking time: 7 hours

1 very large casserole dish (or a slow cooker)

1 leg of lamb, about 4 lb 8 oz in weight
olive oil or goose fat
3 carrots, sliced
2 stalks celery, sliced
3 onions, sliced
5 cloves garlic, finely chopped
6 cups white wine
2 cups water
salt and pepper
1 bouquet garni

Preheat the oven to 240°F.
Take the meat out of the refrigerator at least 30 minutes before it is to go into the oven.
Heat the oil or goose fat in the casserole dish on the hob and brown the lamb all over. Add the vegetables and cook for a few minutes.
Pour in the white wine and water, bring to a boil, season lightly, cover and cook in the oven for about 7 hours, turning the meat from time to time.

Roast pork

In this recipe, the pork is given the same treatment as our leg of lamb. The only difference is that the pork is sealed in order to make the skin nice and crisp. You can also cook it at 240° F and broil it for 10 minutes before serving. The effect will be pretty much the same.

Serves 8–10
Preparation time: 5 minutes
Cooking time: 3 hours

1 roasting pan with a rack
1 mini food processor

1 joint of pork between 2 lb 4 oz–3 lb 5 oz
in weight, either shoulder, boned and rolled,
or leg end, with the skin on
3 cloves garlic
2 tablespoons rosemary
1 teaspoon black pepper
1 tablespoon salt
3–4 tablespoons olive oil

Preheat the oven to 240° F.
Score the pork rind at regular intervals with a sharp knife. Blend the garlic, rosemary, salt, pepper and the oil in the food processor until they form a paste.
Using your hands, coat the meat with this paste, pressing it into the incisions made in the skin.
Cook for about 3 hours, turning the meat from time to time on the rack and basting it regularly with the pan juices. Check every so often to see how it is cooking. Remove excess fat if necessary.
Thirty minutes before serving, take the meat out of the oven, turn the temperature up to 425° F and brown the skin to give a nice, crisp texture on the outside and soft, tender meat on the inside.

Spareribs marinated and roasted in hoisin sauce

Like chili, an ideal dish for adults and children, which can be eaten with the fingers.

Serves 6
Preparation time: 20 minutes
Marinate for 4–5 hours
Cooking time: 2 hours

1 roasting pan

3 lb 5 oz spareribs

For the marinade
2 shallots, finely chopped
1 clove garlic, finely chopped
3 tablespoons rice vinegar
5 tablespoons hoisin sauce (Chinese barbecue sauce)
4 tablespoons water
1 tablespoon soy sauce
white pepper
½ red chili, finely chopped (optional)

Mix the marinade ingredients together in the roasting pan. Coat the ribs all over with it, cover the pan with plastic wrap, and leave for 4 to 5 hours in the refrigerator, turning the meat from time to time.
Preheat the oven to 275° F.
Cook the ribs in the oven for 2 to 2½ hours, turning them from time to time if you think it necessary.
Serve with rice and three tons of paper napkins!

Bolognese sauce
(the real ragù)

Serves 4–6
Preparation time: 15 minutes
Cooking time: 1½ hours

1 large skillet

4 oz bacon cut into pieces, or 1 cup diced
pancetta
2 carrots, cut into rounds
2 onions, finely chopped
2 stalks celery, chopped
1 clove garlic, finely chopped
1½ tablespoons butter
1 lb ground beef
1 cup crushed tomatoes
2 cups canned tomatoes
½ cup red wine
½ cup beef stock
salt and pepper

Heat the butter in the frying pan and brown the
bacon or pancetta, onions, carrots, celery, and
garlic.
When the vegetables have browned, turn up the
heat and gradually brown the meat. Pour in both
the crushed and tinned tomatoes, wine, and stock
and simmer for about 1 hour until the sauce is
nice and thick. Add a little stock if it begins to dry
out. Season to taste.
Serve with fresh pasta and grated Parmesan.

Lasagne

You can use this sauce to make lasagne.

Cook the sheets of lasagne in boiling, salted
water and then lay alternate layers of lasagne and
Bolognese sauce topped with thin slices of
mozzarella in a baking dish. Grate some Parmesan
over the last layer of lasagne and bake in the
oven for 15 minutes at 350° F.

Lucy's extra hot chili

A real family dish. If you're wary of spicy food, go easy on the chili powder.

Serves 8
Preparation time: 15 minutes
Cooking time: 2 hours

1 large stewpot
1 skillet

The vegetables

2 zucchini, coarsely chopped
2 large red bell peppers, coarsely chopped
1 yellow bell pepper, coarsely chopped
olive oil for browning

The meat

3 tablespoons olive oil
2 onions, chopped
2 carrots, chopped
1 tablespoon cumin
1 tablespoon oregano
4 cloves garlic, chopped
3 lb 5 oz ground steak
4 cups beef stock
2 tablespoons tomato paste
1 cup canned chopped tomatoes
½ teaspoon cayenne pepper
2 tablespoons good chili powder
1 tablespoon sugar
1 teaspoon salt
2 teaspoons pepper
3–4 cups canned red kidney beans, rinsed
2 tablespoons chopped parsley
sour cream

Quickly brown the vegetables separately in olive oil in a skillet. Set aside.

Heat the oil in a large stewpot. Add the onions, carrots, cumin, oregano, and garlic. Cook over a moderate heat for 5 minutes.

Turn the heat up, add the meat and brown it. Make sure that it browns nicely. This operation can be done in several stages if necessary.

Add the stock, tomato paste, canned tomatoes, cayenne pepper, chili powder, sugar, salt, and pepper. Simmer uncovered for about 1 hour. When the chili has thickened, add the browned vegetables, kidney beans and parsley, cover and cook for another 10 minutes.

Just before serving, add a spoonful of sour cream. Serve with warm tortillas, more sour cream, salad, and grated Cheddar cheese.

You can leave out the zucchini and bell peppers, but it won't be Lucy's chili!

Rabbit in the dairy

A pale, delicate dish that looks scarcely present-able, because the milk takes on a curdled appearance. However, the very delicate taste of rabbit is not masked by excessively powerful flavors.

Serves 6
Preparation time: 10 minutes
Cooking time: 2 hours

1 casserole dish

3–4 stalks celery, finely chopped
1 leek, white part only, finely chopped
2 strips bacon cut into small pieces, or ¼ cup diced pancetta
1 rabbit, jointed
salt, pepper
2 bay leaves
2 cups milk

Preheat the oven to 350° F.
Place the vegetables with the bacon or pancetta in the bottom of the casserole dish. Lay the rabbit pieces on top, add some salt (but not if the bacon is already salted), pepper, and the bay leaves. Bring the milk to a boil, pour over the rabbit, cover, and cook for about 2 hours.

Nanie's rillettes, or potted pork

Whatever you do, get your butcher to cut up the meat. If you insist on doing it yourself, you may very well get disheartened even before the lengthy cooking process begins!

Preparation time: 5 minutes
Cooking time: 3–4 hours

1 large casserole dish
2 1 lb sterilized preserving jars (see TIP below)

1 lb belly of pork, cubed
1 lb shoulder of pork, cubed
1 onion stuck with 3 cloves
salt and pepper

Place the meat and onion in a casserole dish and cook gently over low heat for 3 to 4 hours, without browning. When the meat is very tender, skim off the fat and reserve it for later.
Remove the onion. Break up the meat with a fork (not a food processor!) in order to prevent the consistency being too fine or too sticky. Season to taste.
Put the meat into sterilized jars and leave to cool completely. Melt the fat and pour a layer over the meat in each jar. Seal the jars and store them in a cool, dry place.
Serve with pickled gherkins or sweet and sour cherries (page 178).

TIP • Before using preserving jars, you should wash and dry them. Then place in a pan of boiling water for several minutes in order to sterilize them. Stand the jars upside down to drain on a clean dish towel. You may also sterilize them in your oven at 225° F for 5 minutes.

Chicken cooked in very good wine (Coq au vin)

I didn't want to believe it, but good wine makes the legendary coq au vin even better. Go for a Burgundy if you can, there's nothing better. But don't tell my husband that his Pommard 1990 ended up in my casseroles!

Serves 5–6
Preparation time: 10 minutes
Cooking time: 3 hours

1 large casserole dish

4 oz (1 stick) butter
4 lb 8 oz chicken pieces
4 oz bacon cut into pieces, or 1 cup diced pancetta
2 cloves garlic
20 small onions
2 tablespoons all-purpose flour
½ glass Armagnac
3½ cups red Burgundy
1 bouquet garni
salt and pepper
7 oz small mushrooms
small pieces of bread and grated Gruyère cheese for the croutons

Heat 2 oz (½ stick) of the butter in a large casserole dish and brown the meat with the bacon or pancetta, garlic, and small onions. Add the flour and cook for several minutes.
Add the Armagnac and flambé it. Mind your eyebrows! Pour on the red wine, add the bouquet garni and season lightly with salt and pepper. Bring to a boil and simmer for about 3 hours. Twenty minutes before the end of the cooking time, fry the mushrooms in the rest of the butter, add them to the chicken and continue cooking. Serve with croutons crisped in the oven with grated Gruyère cheese.

CAKES 'N TEA

How to make a good cup of tea

Here, I freely admit, it's definitely a case of "do what I say, not what I do," since I seldom have the patience to wait for the ideal infusion. Following complaints from my guests, I've done some research. Here are the results.

The first thing to do is to warm the teapot. Pour in some boiling water, replace the lid, and swirl the water around for a few seconds before pouring it down the sink.
While you wait for the water to boil again, put the tea leaves or tea bags (1 per person) into the pot.
Pour on boiling water and leave to brew for the necessary time with the lid on.
For Assam, Earl Grey, Lapsang Souchong, and Darjeeling, leave to brew for 3 to 5 minutes. Oolong needs between 5 and 7 minutes, while green tea will be ready after 1 or 2 minutes.
Never put your teapot in the dishwasher. Just rinse it out. This will preserve the thin layer of tannin that gives it all its individual flavor.
It's best to buy tea in bulk, because it tastes better. After being used for the first time, it will keep for up to 8 months in an airtight jar.

Iced tea

Make some tea, sweeten it to taste and leave it to cool. Add some orange, lemon, or peach juice, together with some slices or chunks of fruit. A few mint leaves will give it a delicious aroma.

Tea loaf

Serves 6–8
Preparation time: 30 minutes
Baking time: 1½ hours
Start steeping the dried fruit the day before

7-inch diameter cake pan
1 wire rack

1½ cups hot tea
2 cups golden raisins
2 cups currants
1 egg
1 teaspoon mixed spice
2 teaspoons baking powder
1 cup (well packed) soft brown sugar
3½ cups all-purpose flour, sifted

Pour the hot tea over the dried fruit and leave to soak overnight.
The next day, preheat the oven to 325° F. Meanwhile, mix together the beaten egg, mixed spice, baking powder, sugar, flour, and the dried fruit. Butter the cake pan and pour in the mixture. Bake for 1½ hours. Remove from the oven and leave to cool for 5 minutes before turning the loaf out on to a wire rack.

TIP • Serve hot or toasted with butter.

Pound cake

Preparation time: 10 minutes
Baking time: 50 minutes

1 electric mixer
1 mixing bowl
1 8-inch diameter cake pan (if you haven't yet bought a flexible silicone cake pan)
1 cake rack

4 eggs
8 oz (2 sticks) butter, plus a knob to grease the pan
1 generous cup sugar
1¾ cups all-purpose flour
1 teaspoon baking powder

Preheat the oven to 350° F.
Butter the pan if you are not using a silicone one.
Cream the butter and sugar until very smooth.
Break the eggs and add to the mixture one at a time while continuing to beat, then add the sifted flour and the baking powder.
Pour the mixture into the cake pan and bake for 45 to 50 minutes.
Leave to cool for a few minutes before turning the cake out of the pan. Leave to cool completely on a rack.

Yogurt cake

An ideal recipe for budding cake-makers who have not yet mastered weights and measures.

Serves 2 adults and 4 proud children
Preparation time: 15 minutes
Baking time: 35 minutes

1 8-inch cake pan
1 mixing bowl
1 electric mixer or elbow grease supplied by assistants

1 knob butter for the cake pan
1 container plain yogurt
2 containers superfine sugar
3 eggs
2 containers all-purpose flour
1 container ground almonds
2 teaspoons baking powder
1 pot heavy cream

Preheat the oven to 350° F.
Butter the cake pan.
Pour the yogurt into a mixing bowl. Rinse out the yogurt pot and use it to measure the other ingredients, beginning with the sugar. Add the sugar to the yogurt, together with the eggs. Beat all the ingredients so that the mixture becomes white and frothy.
Then add the flour, almonds, baking powder, and finally the cream.
Pour the mixture into the cake pan and bake for about 35 minutes.

Madeleines

Makes about 24 madeleines
Preparation time: 10 minutes
Baking time: 30 minutes

1 muffin pan or fluted madeleine pan, preferably a silicone one—otherwise, you risk a nervous breakdown if you have to butter the molds for each new batch!
1 baking sheet

3 eggs
scant ¾ cup sugar
3 oz (¾ stick) salted butter
rind of 1 orange
1⅓ cups all-purpose flour
½ teaspoon baking powder

Preheat the oven to 325° F.
Beat the eggs and sugar until the mixture is very frothy. Add the melted butter, orange rind, flour, and baking powder. Mix well.
Place the pan on the baking sheet, fill each mold two-thirds full and bake in the oven for about 10 minutes.
Make two more batches and eat while still warm.

Lemon cake

Serves 6–8
Preparation time: 15 minutes
Baking time: 45 minutes

1 9-inch cake pan

2 oz (½ stick) unsalted, softened butter
5 tablespoons superfine sugar
2 eggs
½ cup milk
1⅓ cups all-purpose flour
2 teaspoons baking powder
juice and rind of 1 lemon

Preheat the oven to 325° F.
Butter the cake pan.
Cream the butter and 4 tablespoons of the sugar until white and frothy.
Mix together the eggs and milk.
Fold the flour, baking powder, and the egg and milk mixture into the bowl containing the whipped butter and sugar.
Add the lemon rind. Bake in the oven for 45 minutes.
Remove from the oven and soak the cake in the lemon juice sweetened with the remaining sugar.
Leave to cool in the pan.

Orange cake

A miracle—a luxuriously smooth, flavorsome cake, made without flour, that you can serve as a snack or as a dessert, accompanied by a salad of very fresh oranges (page 156).

2 hours to stew the oranges (do this the day before if you wish)
To make the cake: 5 minutes
Baking time: 1 hour

1 pan
1 handheld mixer
1 mixing bowl
1 cake pan

a little butter for greasing the pan
1 orange and 2 clementines (or 2 oranges)
6 eggs
1 teaspoon orange flower water, if you like it
1 teaspoon baking powder
1¼ cups superfine sugar
2½ cups ground almonds
5 or 6 white rough cut sugar cubes, coarsely crushed
juice and rind of 1 lemon

Preheat the oven to 375° F.
Butter the cake pan.
Quarter the oranges, or the oranges and clementines, and remove the seeds. Place in a pan, cover with water, and simmer for about 2 hours. Leave to cool completely before blending to a purée with the mixer.
Beat the eggs with a fork in a mixing bowl. Add the orange purée, orange flower water if you wish, baking powder, superfine sugar, and the ground almonds. Blend thoroughly with the handheld mixer then pour into the cake pan.
Bake in the oven for about 1 hour.
Take the cake out of the oven and leave to cool for a few minutes. Mix the pieces of crushed sugar with the lemon rind and juice. Using a spoon, spread the mixture over the cake and leave to cool completely.
The lemon and sugar syrup will form a delicious crust on the cake.

Boiled cake

A brilliant recipe, in which everything is cooked in a pan before being poured into the cake pan. This is the first *fruit* cake I've dared to take to French friends' houses.

Serves 6–8
Preparation time: 20 minutes
Baking time: 1½ hours

1 cake pan, preferably silicone
1 pan

1 cup water
4 oz (1 stick) butter
1 cup demerara sugar
1¼ cups currants
1¼ cups golden raisins
2 tablespoons mixed spice powder (or any other combination of nutmeg, cinnamon, ginger, and cloves you may have in your cupboards)
1¾ cups all-purpose flour
1 teaspoon baking powder
1 beaten egg

Preheat the oven to 350° F.
If you haven't yet found a silicone cake pan, butter a regular one.
Place all the ingredients in a pan, except for the flour, baking powder, and the egg. Bring gently to a boil and simmer for 20 minutes. Allow to cool completely.
Add the flour, baking powder, and egg and mix well.
Pour the mixture into the cake pan and bake for 1½ hours. Leave the cake to cool in the pan.

Christmas cake

Making an English-style Christmas cake, the recipe for which is handed down from mother to daughter, is a serious business. This recipe comes from my maternal grandmother.

Even if you don't want to serve it on Christmas Day itself, this cake has to be made a long time in advance in order to let it mature and develop its full flavor. Some serious cake-makers bake their Christmas cake at the end of the summer and keep it in a container with an apple so that it remains nice and moist. Since it keeps perfectly well for several months in an airtight container, you will always have something delicious to give any friends who turn up unexpectedly.

Serves a lot of people for a long time
Preparation time: 25 minutes
Baking time: 3 hours

1 deep cake pan, 8 inches in diameter
(springform if possible)
waxed paper

8 oz (2 sticks) unsalted butter, softened
1 packed cup soft brown sugar
4–5 eggs
1¾ cups all-purpose flour
½ cup candied cherries
4 cups currants
2 cups raisins
½ cup citrus rind
⅔ cup ground almonds
½ teaspoon mixed spice
½ teaspoon ground cinnamon
½ teaspoon ground cloves
½ teaspoon ground coriander
1 teaspoon ground ginger
1 small glass Armagnac or brandy

Preheat the oven to 350° F.
Line the cake pan with two layers of waxed paper or baking parchment.
Cream the butter and sugar until the mixture turns pale and frothy. While continuing to beat the mixture, add the whole eggs (whites and yolks) one at a time, and the flour.
Add the fruit, ground almonds, and spices, mix well and pour into the cake pan.
Bake for about 3 hours in the center of the oven, checking it from time to time. The cake should not burn on top and should yield to the touch.
Remove the cake from the oven and leave to cool for a minute or two. Without turning it out of the pan, moisten it with the alcohol, spiking it here and there with a skewer in order to distribute the liquid evenly. Leave to cool completely in the pan.
When the cake has cooled, turn it out of the pan, wrap it carefully in waxed paper and put it in an airtight container.
Traditionally, one week before it is cut, the cake is covered with a layer of almond paste or marzipan and then frosted. However, some people prefer it without…

WARNING • The following recipes on this page contain raw eggs. It is not advisable to serve them to very young children, pregnant women, elderly people or anyone weakened by serious illness. Be sure that the eggs are as fresh as possible. If in any doubt, consult your doctor.

Marzipan (almond paste)
Preparation time: 20 minutes

1 mixing bowl

½ cup superfine sugar
1 cup sifted confectioners' sugar
1¼ cups ground almonds
½ teaspoon vanilla extract
½ teaspoon almond extract
1 teaspoon sherry
1 whole egg + 1 egg yolk, whisked

Mix the superfine and confectioners' sugar with the ground almonds. Add the vanilla and almond extracts, sherry, and the whole egg. Mix thoroughly until you have a thick paste.
On a cold surface sprinkled with a little confectioners' sugar, roll out the marzipan as if it were pastry until it is the same shape as the top of the Christmas cake.
Using a pastry brush, coat one side of the marzipan with the whisked egg yolk and place it coated side down on the Christmas cake so that the marzipan adheres firmly to the cake.
Trim it to shape with a sharp knife.

Royal frosting
Preparation time: 10 minutes

1 mixing bowl

3 cups confectioners' sugar
1 tablespoon lemon juice
2 egg whites, lightly beaten (1 egg is not enough, but 2 is too much, so don't put it all in!)

Sift the sugar carefully, add the lemon juice and about two-thirds of the egg white. Mix until the frosting is thick enough to stay on the cake.
Spread on the cake using a spatula and then a fork, to give a "snow" effect.
Decorate with snowmen, holly leaves, and any other seasonal kitsch you can lay your hands on!

WEEKDAY DINNERS

Any normal person knows that having people to dinner during the week is simply incompatible with modern life — unless you live in a household staffed like Gosford Park. Attempts to do so usually fall into one of the following three categories:

Failed dinner: made up of "quick and easy" dishes, like a roast that turns to rubber or chocolate mousse that ends up the consistency of raw pie crust because of all the chatting that goes on during the preparation.

Successful dinner: you spend all evening shut away in the kitchen just so that you can hold the food aloft triumphantly when it's all ready.

Improvised dinner: this was the opportunity you dreamt of to let your creativity run riot, but did your guests really enjoy the noodles with cognac and cod liver accompanied by fromage frais and chocolate biscuits?

There are those who would have us believe that it's possible to serve up a good dinner in the week by having a vast repertoire of dishes that can be ready in an hour or even 30 minutes. Well, even if it only takes five minutes to cook a swordfish steak in wasabi mayonnaise, where will you find fresh fish near your home when you get back from the office or from school?

There's nothing easier than getting a meal ready in 1 hour flat when you don't have to bath the children, help them with their homework, answer the phone, watch your favorite soap, and make yourself beautiful.

So what's the solution? Get everything ready in advance, of course.

But be careful. There's nothing as likely to unsettle your guests as a host sporting a little smile like Elizabeth Montgomery in "Bewitched" or with a tense expression and chipped nails that make it obvious you've been getting the flaming dinner ready for two days, so they'd better like it or else!

The following recipes are best prepared in advance. You only need to play around with the ingredients for 30 minutes at the most. Time, their most essential ingredient, will do the rest.

Chilled tomato and bell pepper soup with vodka

You prepare it, you mix it, and then you just leave it alone.

Serves 6
Preparation time: 25 minutes
Chilling time: 2 hours

1 mixer
1 large mixing bowl

2 large red bell peppers, cut in half and seeded
2 lb 4 oz very ripe, sweet tomatoes, peeled, seeded, and chopped
1 cucumber, peeled, seeded, and chopped
2 cloves garlic, peeled and chopped
6 tablespoons olive oil
2 tablespoons red wine vinegar
10 ice cubes
1½ cups crushed tomatoes
1 tablespoon chopped basil
1 tablespoon chopped chives
juice of 2 limes
salt and pepper
Worcestershire sauce
vodka or tequila (optional)

Roast or broil the bell peppers (in the oven or over the gas) until the skin becomes blackened and blistered. Put them in a mixing bowl. Cover with plastic wrap and leave to stand for 15 minutes. Condensation will form, which will make them very easy to peel. Put the bell peppers, tomatoes, cucumber, and garlic in the mixer and blend them. Add the olive oil, vinegar, ice cubes, and crushed tomatoes and then mix again. Pour into the serving bowl and add the basil, chives, lime juice, salt, pepper, and Worcestershire sauce. Add a dash or two of vodka or tequila if you wish. Leave to cool in the refrigerator for at least 2 hours. Serve with croutons and salsa.

Salsa

Finely chop 2 shallots, half a red bell pepper and 1 tablespoon of chopped parsley. Mix together and use to garnish the soup just before serving.

Melon and cucumber soup

An ultra-light combination which, served with ice cubes, makes a delicious summer appetizer.

Serves 6–8
Preparation time: 15 minutes
Chilling time: 2 hours

1 food processor

the flesh of 1 very ripe honeydew melon
1 cucumber, peeled and seeded

Mix the two ingredients in the food processor. Pour into small glasses and serve chilled.

Pea and mint soup

You can obviously make this soup with frozen peas, but fresh ones are even better.

Serves 6
Preparation time: 20 minutes
(if the peas are fresh)
Cooking time: 15 minutes
Chilling time: 3–4 hours

1 pan
1 food processor

2 lb 4 oz peas in pod (2–2½ cups shelled)
2 cups water or chicken stock
¾ cup light cream
8–10 mint leaves, chopped
salt and pepper

Shell the peas.
Bring the water or stock to a boil and cook the peas for about 8 minutes (or, if using frozen peas, as instructed on the packet). Add the cream and the chopped mint leaves and let them infuse.
Blend the soup in the food processor, season, and then serve or leave to chill.
If you decide to serve it cold, don't forget to taste it again and adjust the seasoning.

Broccoli and Stilton soup

Serves 6
Preparation time: 15 minutes
Cooking time: 25–30 minutes

1 pan

2 oz (½ stick) butter
1 carrot, cut into rounds
1 small leek, white part only, chopped
1 stalk celery, chopped
1 onion, chopped
6 cups vegetable stock or water
9 cups broccoli florets
¾ cup light cream
1 packed cup crumbled Stilton (or Roquefort, Bleu d'Auvergne or Gorgonzola)
salt and pepper

Melt the butter and brown the vegetables except for the broccoli.
Pour on the stock, bring to a boil and add the broccoli. Cook for about 15 minutes until the broccoli is tender.
Blend, then add the cream and crumbled Stilton into the soup.
Season and serve.

Chestnut soup with chorizo (or salami)

A very filling Spanish soup. Use a strong chorizo or salami if you like spicy food.

Serves 6–8
Preparation time: 10 minutes
Cooking time: 40 minutes

1 large pan

3–4 tablespoons olive oil
9 oz chorizo or salami, sliced
3 cloves garlic
2 onions, finely chopped
2 carrots, peeled and cut into rounds
1 stalk celery, peeled and cut into sticks
1 tablespoon cumin
2 cups canned chopped tomatoes
1 lb 12 oz unsweetened canned chestnuts
6 cups water
a good pinch saffron, infused in ⅔ cup hot water
salt and pepper

Heat the oil and add the chorizo or salami, garlic, onions, carrots, and celery. Cook for 15 to 20 minutes until the ingredients caramelize.
Add the cumin, tomatoes, and chestnuts and cook for a few more minutes.
Add the water and saffron and simmer for 15 minutes. Blend, season, add a little water if the soup is too thick for you and serve with some thick, crusty bread.

My friends' specialties

WE ALL HAVE A DISH THAT TURNS OUT PERFECTLY EVERY TIME WE COOK IT. No need to look at the recipe any more: it's always delicious and everybody loves it. How many times on the way to what's-her-name's house have you said to yourself: "I hope she's made her duck (or stew, curry, charlotte, etc.)"?

If you're one of those who don't relish cooking, you shouldn't feel obliged to regularly vary the dish you serve your guests. Stick with your specialty and change the dessert. It will always go down well (except your raclette in June, Sabine) and you won't have anything to worry about. Here are a few culinary hits from friends who entertain splendidly but don't much like cooking.

Virginie's pot-au-feu (meat and vegetable stew)

Virginie has been showered with compliments since her recipe for chocolate cake appeared in my previous two books. She's still mystified by her new-found fame, since it's not so long ago that she called my husband to find out how to boil an egg!

She is living proof that even the most modest culinary repertoire can include a few small gems that will always hit the spot, even when served for the tenth time. Over the years, they will evolve into real chef's specialties.

Sabine's poule au pot (boiled chicken)

Sabine (super job, husband, three children, house and dog) doesn't have time to cook but she loves to entertain, with flowers, candles, and the works. Her recipe for poule au pot is as legendary as her famous raclettes, which she dishes up unabashed in the middle of June, and her delicious dinners with a Picardy theme.

Emmanuelle's tajine (North African stew)

Every time Emmanuelle entertains, it's a real party. Even if everyday cooking is the least of her concerns, she always manages to delight her friends with simple dishes that leave her time to make herself (very) beautiful. And then there's her husband's collection of Armagnacs…

Valérie's baeckeoffe (stew from the Alsace)

For Valérie and her three sisters, cooking is a family matter to be taken very seriously. A businesswoman, mother of Clément and Pauline, and wife of Nicolas, entertaining is one of her favorite activities. In winter, people say to themselves as they make their way to her house, "I just hope she's made her baeckeoffe…". She puts as much love into this hearty dish, which she always prepares the day before, as her mother and grandmother before her. Beware of imitations!

Meat and vegetable stew (Virginie's pot-au-feu)

Serves 8–10
Preparation time: 20 minutes
Cooking time: 2½ hours

1 casserole dish

6 lb 8 oz stewing beef, cubed
8 carrots, peeled and cut into sticks
8 turnips, peeled and cut in half
8 leeks, white parts only, thickly sliced
3 stalks celery, thickly sliced
3 onions, stuck with cloves
2 bay leaves
1 bouquet garni
10 potatoes, cut into chunks
3 marrow bones (optional)

Fill a large casserole dish with water, put in the meat and bring to a boil. Skim off the excess fat, turn the heat down and simmer for 1 hour.
Add the other ingredients, except for the marrow bones and potatoes, and simmer for another 1½ hours.
Add the potatoes and marrow bones and cook for another half an hour. It's ready!
Serve the meat and vegetables separately with *fleur de sel*, mustard, and gherkins.

North African stew (Emmanuelle's tajine)

Serves 8
Preparation time: 10 minutes
Cooking time: 2 hours

1 earthenware tajine dish

1¼ cups golden raisins
1 cup prunes
3 tablespoons olive oil
1 piece fresh ginger, about the size of your thumb
salt and pepper
8 chicken pieces
3 onions, chopped
1 tablespoon cumin
1 tablespoon turmeric
2 lb 4 oz potatoes, peeled and cut into chunks
3 zucchini, thickly sliced
1 bunch flat-leaf parsley, chopped

Plump up the golden raisins and prunes in hot water. Pour the oil into the tajine dish with the ginger, salt, and pepper. Mix together and cook over a low heat for 5 minutes.
Add the chicken pieces and turn them over in the mixture so that they pick up the flavor. Add the onions and cook everything for 10 to 15 minutes. Then add the cumin and turmeric and mix in thoroughly. Add the potatoes, zucchini, and parsley.
Drain the dried fruit and place it on the top. Cook over a low heat for about 1 hour.
Add water while the chicken is cooking if the tajine starts to dry out.

Boiled chicken (Sabine's poule au pot)

Serves 6–8
Preparation and cooking time the day before: 1¾ hours
Preparation and cooking time before serving: 30 minutes

1 large casserole dish

1 free-range chicken, 3 lb 4 oz–4 lb in weight
1 onion, stuck with cloves
salt and pepper
3 carrots, peeled and cut into sticks
4 turnips, peeled and cut in half
1 leek

To serve

rice
3 tablespoons all-purpose flour
4 oz (1 stick) butter
3 egg yolks
juice of ½ lemon
3 tablespoons cream

The day before, put the whole chicken and the onion into a large casserole dish, season with salt and pepper, cover with water, and bring to a boil. Cook over a low heat for 45 minutes.
Add the vegetables and simmer for 45 minutes longer.
Leave to cool completely so that you will be able to skim the fat off the stock the next day.
Thirty minutes before serving, drain off sufficient stock to cook rice for 8 people. Reheat the chicken and vegetables in the stock, then put them on the serving dish and keep them warm.
Make a roux with 3 tablespoons of flour and the stick of butter and gradually pour in the stock in order to obtain a thick sauce. Just before serving, add 3 egg yolks, some lemon juice, and 3 tablespoons of cream.
Reheat gently to cook the egg yolks but making sure that the sauce does not boil, and serve with the chicken, rice, and vegetables.

Stew from the Alsace (Valérie's baeckeoffe)

Baeckeoffe is an Alsatian dish prepared in a large clay terrine but a heavy casserole dish or slow cooker will do just as well.

Serves an entire army
Marinating time: overnight
Preparation time: 15 minutes
Cooking time: 3 hours

1 very large casserole dish or a slow cooker

1 lb 10 oz stewing or braising beef, cubed
1 lb 10 oz shoulder of lamb, cubed
1 lb 10 oz pork shoulder, cubed
6 lb 8 oz potatoes, peeled and cut into ¼-inch slices
1 lb onions, chopped
thyme
pepper

For the marinade

8 oz bacon cut into pieces or diced pancetta
4 cups Riesling
1 carrot, cut into rounds
1 onion, chopped
1 clove garlic, crushed
2 cloves
3 bay leaves
2 tablespoons parsley
salt and pepper

Mix all the marinade ingredients together, pour over the three portions of meat in seperate bowls, and leave overnight.
Preheat the oven to 350° F.
Place a layer of potatoes on the bottom of the dish. Sprinkle with pieces of bacon or pancetta, then add thyme, salt, and pepper. Cover with a layer of pork. Add a layer of potatoes and the onions and then a layer of lamb. Cover with another layer of potatoes and finish with a layer of beef.
Pour on the marinade and cook for about 3 hours.

Lamb shanks with chickpeas and ras el hanout

Serves 4
Preparation time: 20 minutes
Cooking time: 2½ hours

1 cast-iron casserole dish

3 tablespoons olive oil
4 lamb shanks
2 onions, finely chopped
2 cloves garlic, finely chopped
1 piece fresh ginger the size of your thumb,
peeled and finely chopped (optional)
1 lb carrots, cut into rounds
2–3 tablespoons ras el hanout (Moroccan
spice mix)
2 cups canned chopped tomatoes
1 15 oz can chickpeas (garbanzo beans)
1 cup no-soak apricots
¾ cup no-soak prunes
2 tablespoons honey
1 cup blanched almonds
fresh cilantro if available
salt and pepper

Preheat the oven to 325° F.
Heat the olive oil in the casserole dish and brown
the meat all over. Discard the oil if it has become
too blackened.
In the same pan, adding a little oil if necessary, fry
the onions, garlic, ginger, carrots and ras el
hanout for a few minutes. Add the tomatoes and
stir everything together.
Cook for a minute or two and then add some
water (about 3 cups) until the meat is half
covered. Bring to a boil and simmer uncovered for
5 to 10 minutes. Cover and cook in the oven for
2 hours.

Thirty minutes before serving, add the chickpeas,
season with salt and pepper and continue to cook
in the oven or on the hob.
Just before serving, add the fruit and honey.
Brown the almonds in a frying pan and sprinkle
them over the dish. Add a little fresh cilantro if
you have some to hand.

You can get everything ready the day before,
stopping before you add the chickpeas. Just start
cooking again half an hour before you want to
serve up.

Irish stew

One of the national dishes of Ireland: just lamb cooked over a low heat with potatoes, onions, parsley, and thyme. The luxury version includes carrots and sometimes even leeks.

Serves 4–6
Preparation time: 10 minutes
Cooking time: 2 hrs

1 large casserole dish

1 lb waxy potatoes, thinly sliced
1 lb 10 oz neck of lamb, cut into pieces
2 onions, thinly sliced
1 tablespoon chopped parsley
1 tablespoon thyme leaves
salt and pepper

Preheat the oven to 325° F.
Place alternate layers of potatoes, lamb, onions, and herbs in the casserole dish, seasoning as you go. Finish with a layer of potatoes and press gently to pack everything down nicely.
Pour on 1¼ cups of water, cover, and cook in the oven for about 2 hours.

Lamb stew, slightly burnt, with sun-dried tomatoes

Dried in the sun and/or preserved in oil, dried tomatoes of all sorts have invaded supermarket shelves. The ones in the photo opposite were completely dry. They were rehydrated in the cooking liquid. Avoid ready-made sauces, which are often too strongly flavored.

Serves 6
Preparation time: 10 minutes
Cooking time: 1½ hours

1 large casserole dish

2 tablespoons olive oil
2 cloves garlic, crushed
2 onions, finely chopped
12 pieces neck of lamb (or 6 lamb chops)
2 cups white wine
thyme and/or rosemary
10 pieces sun-dried tomato
salt and pepper

Heat the oil and brown the garlic and onions. Brown the lamb—this is where you start to burn it a bit—then pour on the wine and add the thyme, salt, and pepper. Simmer for about 1½ hours.
At this point, you can try to make the lamb stick a little to the bottom of the pan or, even better, wait until you reheat the dish to carry out this operation.

Thai pork curry

Curry is an excellent example of food that improves if forgotten for a while. Left to cool and then reheated, the spices have time to develop their full flavor. Lemon grass is not always easy to find if you don't have an Asian grocer in your neighborhood. It does freeze very well, however, if bought fresh. Otherwise, you'll have to make do with the dried version or lemon grass paste in a jar.

Serves 4–6
Preparation time: 45 minutes
Cooking time: 1 hour

1 food processor
1 heavy-based pan or cast-iron casserole dish

1 lb 10 oz pork suitable for sautéing, cut into pieces
(Do not use meat without any fat. The fat makes the curry smoother and tastier. Shoulder is the best cut.)
2 tablespoons lime juice
1 tablespoon soy sauce
1¾ cups canned coconut milk
½ cup water
1 bunch fresh cilantro, chopped

The curry paste
1 red chili (optional)
1 piece ginger or galangal, about the size of your thumb
2 sticks fresh lemon grass or 2 tablespoons dried lemon grass soaked for 20 minutes in lukewarm water
2 onions, finely chopped
6 cloves garlic, finely chopped
1 tablespoon ground coriander seeds
2 tablespoons ground cumin
1 tablespoon turmeric

Make the curry paste by mixing all the ingredients in a food processor.
Mix the paste, meat, lime juice and soy sauce together in a bowl and leave to marinate for about 1 hour.
Put the meat and the paste into a heavy-based pan or casserole dish and brown the meat, starting over a low heat so that it gives off a little of its fat. Then turn the heat up until the meat begins to dry out and turn brown. Add the coconut milk and ½ cup of water and simmer for about 50 minutes.
Stir well and, depending on your taste, either add water or coconut milk, or reduce the liquid to make it thicker. Adjust the seasoning to taste. Serve with basmati rice sprinkled with fresh cilantro.

Guinness stew

Serves 4
Preparation time: 15 minutes
Cooking time: 1½–2 hours

1 large cast-iron casserole dish

1 tablespoon butter
1 tablespoon olive oil
2 slices bacon, cut into large pieces
2 onions, chopped
1 lb 10 oz braising steak, cubed and with
the fat trimmed off
2 tablespoons all-purpose flour
2 cups beef stock
1¼ cups Guinness (or any other Irish stout)
1 bouquet garni
2 carrots, sliced
salt and black pepper

Heat the oil and butter in a large cast-iron
casserole dish and brown the bacon, onions, and
meat for a few minutes. Sprinkle on the flour and
cook for 1 minute.
Remove from the heat and pour on the stock and
beer. Stir and bring to a boil, stirring constantly.
Add the bouquet garni and the sliced carrots.
Cover and simmer over a low heat for 1½ to
2 hours.
When you are ready to serve, remove the bouquet
garni and check the seasoning. Serve with boiled
potatoes.

Breast of veal with roast carrots

A very simple recipe for a very tasty cut of meat.

Serves 6
Preparation time: 20 minutes
Cooking time: 2 hours

1 large casserole dish

2 tablespoons olive oil
2 carrots, cut into rounds
4 oz smoked bacon cut into pieces or 1 cup diced pancetta,
2 onions, finely chopped
3 lb 5 oz breast of veal, rolled and tied with string
1 glass water
salt and pepper

Preheat the oven to 350° F.
Heat the oil in the casserole dish and brown the carrots, bacon or pancetta, and onions. Add the veal and brown it thoroughly. Add the water, season lightly with salt and pepper, cover and cook in the oven for about 2 hours. Serve with roast carrots (page 136).

Steak and kidney pie

Serves 6
Preparation time: 25 minutes
Cooking time: 2 hours

1 large casserole dish
1 gratin dish

3 oz (¾ stick) butter
2 tablespoons olive oil
2 onions, chopped
3 carrots, cut into rounds
1 lb 8 oz stewing steak, cubed
9 oz ox (beef) or lambs' kidneys, cut into pieces
2 tablespoons all-purpose flour
2¾ cups beef stock or water
1 tablespoon tomato paste
1 bay leaf
6 oz mushrooms, quartered
salt and pepper
Worcestershire sauce
12 oz pie crust dough
1 beaten egg

Heat the oil and butter in a large casserole dish and brown the onions and carrots. Add the meat and seal it all over before adding the flour. Cook for a few minutes and then pour on the stock—or water—to which you have added the tomato paste, bay leaf, and the mushrooms. Half-cover with the lid and cook for 1½ to 2 hours over a low heat. The sauce should be considerably reduced and thick.
Add the salt, pepper, and Worcestershire sauce. Place the meat in the gratin dish and leave to cool for a few minutes.
Preheat the oven to 425° F.
Roll out the pie crust dough and generously cover the dish filled with meat. Stick down the edges with the beaten egg. Seal the sides tightly and, using a brush, glaze the crust with beaten egg to give it a pretty color. Put the dish in the oven and cook for about 30 minutes.

Pie crust

Preparation time: 10 minutes
Refrigeration time: 2 hours

1 food processor

2 cups all-purpose flour
4 oz (1 stick) + 1 tablespoon chilled butter
3–4 tablespoons very cold water

Put the flour and butter in a food processor and mix together until you have a crumbly dough. Pour in the water and mix for a few more seconds. Press into a ball and wrap in plastic wrap.
Place in the refrigerator for 2 hours.

If you want to use this pie crust recipe to make a sweet tart or pie, add 2 tablespoons of superfine sugar.

Osso bucco

A great classic. Serve with fresh pasta or rice.

Serves 6
Preparation time: 10 minutes
Cooking time: 2 hours

1 casserole dish

6 pieces shin of veal
1 tablespoon all-purpose flour
4 tablespoons olive oil
2 onions, chopped
1 clove garlic
2 carrots, cut into rounds
2 cups dry white wine
2 cups canned tomatoes
rind of an orange
1 tablespoon thyme leaves
salt and pepper

Roll the pieces of veal in the flour. Brown in the oil, then add the onions, garlic and carrots. Pour on the wine and tomatoes and add the orange rind and thyme. Season with salt and pepper, cover and simmer for 1½ to 2 hours.

PEOPLE HAVE OFTEN MADE FUN OF MY IMMODERATE PASSION FOR CHICKEN. For many years, every time I went to a restaurant I went through agony trying to choose meat or fish from the menu. At home, I had to use all my willpower to cook something other than chicken.

And then, one day, I was given *Le Grand Livre de la Volaille* (The Big Book of Poultry) by Georges Blanc and I realized I wasn't the only one to experience this unbounded love.

With the following recipes, my coming-out is complete. From now on, I'm going to dedicate my life to writing my greatest masterpiece, *The Big Book of Chicken in Cream Sauce with Mashed Potatoes.*

Quick chicken

Sometimes, you're just in too much of a hurry to
track down morally irreproachable products, those
wonders covered with labels guaranteeing origin,
quality, organic production, and so on. Here's a
recipe whose ingredients will be found in the most
modest of local grocery stores. For those evenings
when a delivery of sushi or pizza is absolutely out
of the question…

Serves 4
Preparation time: 5 minutes
Cooking time: 1½ hours

1 casserole dish

2 oz (½ stick) butter
4 chicken thighs
5 shallots, finely chopped
1 bottle white wine
3–4 tablespoons heavy cream

Preheat the oven to 350° F.
Heat the butter and brown the chicken and
shallots. When the chicken is brown all over, pour
on the wine, season lightly, cover and cook in the
oven for 1 to 1½ hours.
Before serving, add the cream and allow the
sauce to thicken.
If you absolutely insist on displaying your
unbridled exoticism, add a little tarragon or a
tablespoon of mustard at the end of the cooking
time.
Serve with tagliatelle.

Garlic chicken

In theory, roast garlic is easily digestible and shouldn't leave you with camel's breath (which would be absolutely dreadful of course!). Unfortunately, one Wednesday evening, I didn't give this dish quite enough time to cook and my guests, a banker and his headhunter wife, couldn't open their mouths in polite company until the following Monday.
Sorry Fred and Kath…

Serves 6
Preparation time: 10 minutes
Cooking time: 1½ hours

1 casserole dish

salt and pepper
40 garlic cloves, with the ends cut off but the last layer of skin still on
1 nice-looking free-range chicken, weighing between 3 lb 5 oz and 4 lb 8 oz
3–4 tablespoons olive oil
2 French sticks or baguettes
sea salt

Preheat the oven to 350° F.
Put some salt, pepper and a few cloves of the garlic in the chicken cavity. Heat the oil in the casserole dish and brown the chicken all over. Brown the rest of the garlic cloves for a few minutes, then pour on some water until it reaches half-way up the chicken's legs. Cover and cook in the oven for 1½ hours without disturbing.
Five minutes before serving, cut the French bread into small croutons. Pour a few drops of olive oil over the bread and bake in the oven until golden. Carry the casserole dish and the croutons to the table and let your guests enjoy the delicious aroma that will pervade the room when you lift off the lid.
Crush the garlic cloves on to the croutons. Serve with a crispy salad.

Squab chickens (poussins) roasted in lemon, thyme, garlic, and butter

I feel cruel when I serve these poor little chickens. However, half a poussin is the perfect portion. It has white meat, a leg, and an "oyster"—the choice piece of meat in the front hollow of the side bone.

Serves 6
Preparation time: 10 minutes
Cooking time: 2 hours

1 roasting pan

3 squab chickens
rind and juice of 2 lemons
2 cloves garlic, finely chopped
1 tablespoon thyme leaves
3 tablespoons olive oil
2 tablespoons butter
salt and pepper

Preheat the oven to 300° F.
Mix together the rind and lemon juice, garlic, thyme, and olive oil and rub vigorously into the squabs' skin. Leave a little of the mixture in the birds' cavity and put the remainder in the roasting pan.
Place the squabs in the pan and roast in the oven for 3 hours.
Season just before serving.
Mix the butter, and possibly a little water, into the pan juices, which by then will have reduced to a delicious caramelized syrup.

Slow roast duck

This is my own interpretation of one of British chef Jamie Oliver's recipes (how cute is he?!). He's an idol to my children and an absolute mystery to my husband. *Jamie, we love you!*

Serves 6 (A duck may look nice and plump at first sight, but there really isn't much to get your teeth into underneath.)
Preparation time: 5 minutes
Cooking time: 2 hours

1 roasting pan with a wire rack on which to place the ducks

2 ducks
2 cloves garlic
olive oil
salt and pepper
1 onion

Preheat the oven to 375° F.
Rub the ducks all over with the peeled garlic, a little oil, and some salt. Put half an onion in each duck cavity. Roast for 1 hour, then turn the oven down to 300°F. Cook for another hour. From time to time, drain off the fat that accumulates in the roasting pan. The ducks will be crisp on the outside and soft on the inside.
Serve with braised red cabbage (page 140).

Venison casserole

Traditionally made with wild boar but venison is easier to come by. Alternatively you could use pork shoulder or leg.

Serves 6
Preparation time: 15 minutes
Marinating time: 24 hours
Cooking time: 1½ hours

1 cast-iron casserole dish

4 lb 8 oz venison (or pork), cut into large cubes
2 tablespoons butter
5 tablespoons olive oil
2 tablespoons all-purpose flour
4 cups red wine

The marinade
2 onions, chopped
1 carrot, cut into rounds
2 cloves garlic, crushed
1 bouquet garni
salt and pepper

Mix all the marinade ingredients with 2 cups of the red wine and marinate the meat for 24 hours. Remove the pieces of meat from the marinade and dry them on kitchen towel. Put the marinade through a sieve, crushing the vegetable pieces in order to extract the flavor.
Heat the butter and oil in the casserole dish and brown the meat so that it is well sealed all over. Add the flour and cook for a little longer, taking care not to burn the meat or the roux (the mixture of fat and flour).
Deglaze the pan by pouring on the marinade and scraping the bottom in order to loosen the cooked flour. Cover the meat with the rest of the wine, put the lid on and simmer for about 1½ hours.
Serve with boiled potatoes and mashed turnips.

Pheasant (or guinea fowl) with foie gras

A festive dish that can be fully prepared in advance.

Serves 8
Preparation time: 25 minutes
Cooking time: 1½ hours

1 roasting pan
2 cake pans
1 large pan
1 skillet

2 pheasants (or 1 guinea fowl)
salt and pepper
2 onions
2 green cabbages
2 oz (½ stick) butter
4 oz bacon, cut into pieces, or 1 cup diced pancetta
7 oz part-cooked foie gras

Preheat the oven to 425° F.
Season each pheasant (or guinea fowl) with salt and pepper and stuff with a peeled onion. Roast for about 1 hour.
Remove the bird(s) from the oven and leave them to cool long enough for you to be able to take off all the flesh without burning yourself, and cut it into bite-sized pieces. Put the pan juices to one side.
Slice the cabbage and cook in salted water for about 30 minutes. Drain and mix in the butter. Brown the pieces of bacon or pancetta in the skillet. Finely chop the foie gras.
Mix the cabbage, bacon or pancetta, foie gras, and meat with the pan juices. Season with salt and pepper. Place everything in the cake pans. Keep warm before turning out of the pans or leave to cool and then reheat for 15 minutes at 350° F before serving.

Variation

You could add some apple to the cabbage 15 minutes before the end of the cooking time.

Roast venison

You know the problems I have with any dish requiring precise timing in the middle of a meal.
You'll have to serve this one after a starter that will absorb your guests for the whole time the meat is cooking. If you make sure that all the other parts of the meal require a minimum of attention, this roast will be
perfect for a Christmas or New Year's Eve dinner.

Serves 6–8
Preparation time: 10 minutes
Marinating time: 24 hours
Cooking time: 20–30 minutes

1 roasting pan

1 venison joint, about 2 lb 4 oz in weight
(if you can't buy venison, use lamb instead)

The marinade

1 red onion, chopped
1 shallot, chopped
1 clove garlic, chopped
5 tablespoons olive oil
1 tablespoon juniper berries, coarsely crushed
2 tablespoons coriander seeds, coarsely crushed
1 tablespoon thyme and rosemary, mixed and
chopped
juice and rind of 1 lemon
5 tablespoons port
black pepper

For the sauce

⅔ cup beef stock (page 186)
2–3 tablespoons redcurrant jelly

Mix all the ingredients for the marinade. Put the
joint in a dish and pour on the marinade, making
sure that the whole joint is covered. Cover with
plastic wrap and leave to marinate overnight in
the refrigerator. Turn the meat before going to
bed and once more in the morning when you get
up.
Preheat the oven to 425° F.
While your guests are fighting over the seating
plan, run to the kitchen, take the meat out of the
marinade and dry it on kitchen towel.
Heat a little olive oil in a skillet and brown the
meat all over.
Put the rest of the marinade through a fine sieve,
add the stock and reduce it while the meat is
cooking.
Place the meat in the roasting pan, moisten it
with a little of the marinade and cook for 20 to
30 minutes depending on how you like it.
Take the opportunity to rejoin your guests and
enjoy the starter.
Take the meat out of the oven and leave to stand
while you prepare the sauce.
Before serving, pour the pan juices into the sauce
and add one or two tablespoons of redcurrant
jelly.
Delicious with roast pears and mashed potatoes
with truffles and butter.

LEFTOVERS

Leftovers are perhaps the least glamorous aspect of cooking. Some may think that the mere fact that they have leftovers in their refrigerator represents failure. What went wrong? Did I miscalculate? Was it not very good?

However, you and I know very well that the remains of slow cooked, reheated, preserved, and infused dishes are the best bits.

The bottom of the dish, the burnt and sticky bits, the gravy, or pan juices—these are all good reasons for insisting on being left alone to clear up the kitchen. That way, you can have a few private moments scraping out the remains of the stew or spooning up the last remnants of the custard sauce. Yes, that's right—the bit at the bottom, where all the vanilla seeds collect.

When there are a lot of leftovers, or you've made large quantities deliberately in order to have some leftovers, the original dish has to be totally transformed in order to avoid the feeling of déjà vu. Here are a few suggestions for Sunday evening that favor small stomachs over large trash cans.

A few ideas for using up cold meat in some unusual but delicious salads.

Poached ham and green vegetable salad with mustard and honey vinaigrette

Gently simmer some green beans and peas in a little water. Cut some fennel and Granny Smith apples into very thin strips. Peel and seed a cucumber. Serve with a vinaigrette made of olive oil, Meaux mustard, and honey.

Roast duck and grilled plum salad with chili sauce

Grill some red plums for about 20 minutes. Mix them with the duck, cut into pieces, and some Chinese chili sauce, which you will find on the exotic products shelves of your supermarket. Don't worry, it's not very strong.

Beef and lentil salad with lemon, cumin, walnuts, flat-leaf parsley, and olive oil

Mix together the lemon juice and finely chopped parsley with olive oil and cumin.
Combine this mixture with some cooked lentils and some cooked beef cut into pieces. Season and sprinkle with chopped walnuts.

Chicken, orange and tomato salad with almonds, basil, and mint

Peel and chop the oranges, saving their juice. Slice some tomatoes. Cut the chicken into pieces. Sauté some almonds in a skillet. Make a vinaigrette with olive oil, orange juice and finely chopped basil and mint.
Mix everything together, season and sprinkle with the almonds.

Pasta cooked in stock

No recipes, just a reminder not to overlook the excellent fresh and dried pasta available in the shops.

If you've used the recipes on the preceding pages, you'll have made pints and pints of delicious stock. Why not use it to cook ravioli or fresh gnocchi?

Parmesan rind soup

All the flavour of Parmesan is concentrated in the rind. You can combine it with celery, leeks, or potatoes to make a very aromatic soup. So there's no reason to throw away those rinds!

Serves 4
Preparation time: 5 minutes
Cooking time: 30 minutes

1 food processor
1 pan

6 cups chicken or vegetable stock (or if you have no stock already made, 6 cups water with a sliced carrot, a chopped onion, and some thyme or bay leaves)
4 stalks celery, peeled or 2 leeks, white parts only, roughly chopped
5 oz, or about 1 cup parmesan rinds
salt and pepper
2 tablespoons cream (optional)

Bring the stock or water to a boil and throw in the vegetables and parmesan rinds. Cook over a gentle heat for 30 minutes. Remove the parmesan rinds, which will have swelled up and disintegrated slightly. Blend the soup in the food processor, season, add the cream if you wish, and serve.

Lamb, zucchini, feta, mint, dill, and olive oil on pita

Sauté some zucchini slices in very hot olive oil, then set them aside to drain on kitchen.towel. Chop the mint and warm a pita bread for 1 minute in the microwave or oven. Stuff the bread with lamb, warm zucchini, crumbled feta cheese, mint, and dill. Add salt, pepper, and olive oil.

David's club sandwich

When we got home from school, my little brother and I used to make club sandwiches in silence. The bacon had to be lightly broiled and well drained of excess fat, the tomatoes sliced very finely and the chicken not too thickly cut. Just the right amount of very white mayonnaise had to be measured out, so that the sandwiches stayed nice and moist but without everything running all over our school uniforms. All the ingredients had to be ready before we toasted the white bread, so that it remained warm and crusty.
Unfortunately, as I'm sure you'll understand, I can't give you the exact recipe for this sandwich, which requires years of experience to make. Practice makes perfect.

Beef, beet, apple, and horseradish butter on farmhouse bread

Mix a teaspoon of ready-made horseradish relish and 2 oz (½ stick) of salted butter. Season with pepper.
Toast two thick slices of good fresh bread. Spread the butter and then place the beef on one of the slices of bread. Add some strips of cooked beet and Granny Smith apple and then place the second slice of bread on top to complete the sandwich.

Pork, pineapple, cucumber, chili, and scallion wraps

Cut the cucumber into sticks and finely chop the chili and scallions. Mix with the other ingredients, moistening everything a little with some rice vinegar. Roll everything up in a rice flour pancake or tortilla.

Open sandwiches

Top a slice of good bread, toasted or plain, with any of the preparations described on page 178 (chutneys, relishes, and preserves).

Gratin dauphinois

Serves 4–6
Preparation time: 25 minutes
Cooking time: 1½ hours

1 gratin dish

1 clove garlic
2 oz (½ stick) unsalted butter
2 lb 4 oz waxy potatoes, peeled and
thinly sliced
salt and pepper
grated nutmeg
1 cup milk
1 cup light cream

Preheat the oven to 350° F.
Rub the dish with the peeled clove of garlic and
then grease it with half of the butter.
Place the potatoes in layers in the dish.
Season with salt and pepper and sprinkle each
layer lightly with grated nutmeg.
Mix together the milk and cream, warm and pour
over the potatoes.
Cube the rest of the butter and sprinkle it over
the top.
Cook in the oven for 1¼ hours.
Increase the heat to 400° F and leave to cook for
another 15 minutes in order to brown the top
nicely.

Gratin savoyard

The ingredients and procedure are the same as for
the gratin dauphinois. Just add 1–2 cups grated
Gruyère cheese between the layers of potatoes
and on top of the gratin.

Mixed vegetable gratin

This is one of the best ways of livening up a rather
dull Sunday evening.

Preparation time: 5 minutes
Cooking time: 15–20 minutes

1 gratin dish

leftover cooked vegetables (ratatouille,
potatoes, broccoli, carrots, leeks, Brussels
sprouts, etc.)
light cream
a little bacon or boiled ham if you have some
left over
1 cup cheese (e.g. Parmesan, Cheddar, Gruyère,
mozzarella, ricotta) cut into pieces
salt and pepper

Preheat the oven to 400° F.
Mix all the ingredients together, keeping back a
little Cheddar, Parmesan or Gruyère to grate over
the top. Place them in the gratin dish and cook in
the oven for 15 to 20 minutes.

Chicken crumble with leeks and sage

Apply the same principle to using up leftovers of
pork, Christmas turkey, and even vegetables.

Serves 4–6
Preparation time: 15 minutes
Cooking time: 25 minutes

1 skillet
1 gratin dish

2 tablespoons olive oil
4 oz (1 stick) butter
1 lb leeks, white parts only, sliced
1 tablespoon sage, chopped
2–3 cups leftover roast chicken, cut into pieces
1½ cups light cream
salt and pepper
1 cup all-purpose flour
5 tablespoons oat flakes (porrige oats)
¾ cup grated Cheddar or Parmesan cheese

Preheat the oven to 400° F.
Heat the olive oil and one-quarter of the butter in
a skillet and sauté the leeks and sage over a
gentle heat until well cooked. Add the chicken
and the cream and bring to a boil. Season and
place in a gratin dish.
To make the crumble, rub the flour and the rest
of the butter together with your fingers until the
mixture resembles breadcrumbs. Add the oat
flakes, salt, pepper, and cheese and spread the
mixture over the leeks and chicken.
Cook for 20 to 25 minutes, or until the crumble
topping is nice and golden. Simple!

Tomato clafouti

Serves 4-6
Preparation time: 45 minutes
Cooking time: 30 minutes

1 gratin dish

1 recipe small roast tomatoes (page 138)
1 tbsp olive oil
salt and pepper
4 whole eggs + 1 egg yolk
1¾ cups light cream
1¼ cups milk
2 tbsp all-purpose flour, sifted
1¼ cups Parmesan cheese, freshly grated

Preheat the oven to 350° F.
Chop the tomatoes and sprinkle with olive oil.
Season with salt and pepper. Drain if necessary
and transfer to a gratin dish.
Beat the eggs and the yolk with the milk and
cream. Add the sifted flour and Parmesan cheese
and season to taste. Pour over the tomatoes and
bake for about 30 minutes.

Cottage pie deluxe

Let yourself go, stop pretending that the only thing this dish is good for is using up leftovers. You and I know very well that it's actually a rather dubious excuse for combining various kinds of flavorsome (and miraculously preground) meat with delicious mashed potatoes. Here are a few over-the-top suggestions…

1 To make the meat more succulent, don't hesitate to add some of the pan juices—or even some duck fat if you are using duck—when you place it in the bottom of the dish.

2 Cut the meat into very small pieces. Be up to date for once. Fashion is regressing. Anything that even faintly resembles the boiled beef of our childhood will go down well.

3 Add some layers of unusual ingredients: pine nuts, almonds, broiled walnuts, stewed dried fruit, spices, foie gras, onions, shallots, preserved garlic, or mashed peas, carrots, apples, pears etc.

4 I will never reveal the amount of butter and cream I put in my mashed potatoes. I always use light cream for this recipe.

5 Always season the mashed potatoes properly and do not stint on either the quantity or quality of the grated cheese, whether it be Cheddar, Parmesan, or Gruyère.

Some interesting combinations:

Oxtail, preserved garlic and shallots, mashed potatoes with horseradish.

Belly of pork, fried mushrooms and bacon, mashed potatoes.

Roast lamb, toasted pine nuts and almonds, spicy mashed potatoes.

Roast duck, apple or pear purée, mashed potatoes.

Poached ham, poached peaches, mashed potatoes and peas.

Chicken, broiled corn on the cob, mashed potatoes, and fried onions.

Bread and butter pudding

A childhood favorite and a real comfort food. It's even better when you replace the stale bread with croissants, milk bread with raisins, or brioche. The "butter" in the name alludes to the butter traditionally spread on the bread before the pudding was cooked. It's up to you whether or not to follow tradition…

Serves 6
Preparation time: 10 minutes
Standing time: 20 minutes
Cooking time: 40–50 minutes

1 electric mixer
1 gratin dish

4–5 croissants or 5–6 slices brioche
or 6–7 slices white sandwich bread
or 5–6 pieces of stale French bread
2 whole eggs and 3 egg yolks
4 tablespoons sugar
2 cups milk
1 vanilla bean
2 cups light cream

Preheat the oven to 325° F.
Cut the bread (or the croissants, brioche, etc.) into pieces and place them in the dish.
Beat the eggs and sugar until the mixture becomes pale and frothy.
Meanwhile, bring the milk and cream to a boil with the vanilla bean split in two lengthwise.
Pour the hot milk and cream over the eggs and stir vigorously. Scrape out the inside of the vanilla bean and add the seeds to the custard. Pour the custard over the bread and leave to soak for 15 minutes.
Put in the oven and cook for 40 to 50 minutes.
Serve warm or cold.

EASY SIDE DISHES

Rainbow bell peppers

Make the most of the colors at a time when you can buy three or four different colored bell peppers, red onions too.

They are delicious roasted, if you just forget about them alongside your joint in a low oven. They can also be served crisp, cooked in a hotter oven.

Serves 6
Cooking time: 40 minutes to 1½ hours depending on oven temperature

1 ovenproof dish

4 or 5 different colored bell peppers, seeded and sliced
2 red onions, chopped
1 piece of fresh root ginger (about the size of your thumb), grated
2 cloves of garlic, finely chopped
rind and juice of 2 limes
rind and juice of 1 lemon
2 tablespoons olive oil
salt, pepper

Place all the ingredients in an ovenproof dish, mix well with the fingers, and cook for 45 minutes at 350° F—or longer in a cooler oven.

MANY VEGETABLES BENEFIT FROM SLOW COOKING IN THE OVEN ALONGSIDE THE DISH WITH WHICH THEY WILL EVENTUALLY BE EATEN. With the aid of a little olive oil, a long stay in the oven will bring out their flavor and impart a slightly caramelized taste. Carrots, broccoli, cauliflower and parsnips will need almost 1 hour at 300°F to become very soft and tender. Potatoes should be parboiled for 10 minutes before they are put in the oven.

Bell peppers, eggplant and zucchini will be transformed after half an hour. Tomatoes are worth a special mention (page 138). They're absolutely wonderful sprinkled with a little sugar and baked in olive oil for 2 to 3 hours at 300°F.

Roast vegetables

Serves 6
Preparation time: 10 minutes
Cooking time: 45 minutes

2 tomatoes
1 eggplant
1 or 2 bell peppers
1 or 2 zucchini
1 red or white onion
4–5 tablespoons olive oil
1 or 2 cloves garlic
1 teaspoon thyme leaves
1 sprig rosemary
salt and pepper

Chop the vegetables into large cubes and sprinkle lightly with olive oil. Roast them in the oven with the other ingredients at 350° F for about 1 hour. Turn them several times until they are well browned or even blackened in places.

Roast onions, garlic, and shallots

Roast the vegetables in an ovenproof dish alongside a joint of meat or other dish that you are cooking slowly in the oven.

You can cook them either in their skins—in which case the onions will need about 50 minutes at 300° F, the shallots about 40 minutes, and the garlic about 25 minutes—or peeled and sprinkled with olive oil and a little sugar.

Eggplant in honey and pepper

Serves 6
Cooking and preparation time: 15 minutes
1 night in the refrigerator

1 frying pan

2 tablespoons honey
3 tablespoons white wine vinegar
5 tablespoons water
2 eggplants, cut into thin slices about ¼ inch thick
4–5 tablespoons olive oil
salt and black pepper

Boil the honey, vinegar, and water together for a few minutes. Leave to cool.
Season the sliced eggplants with salt and pepper. Heat the oil in a skillet and sauté the sliced eggplants for a few minutes on each side.
Place the slices in a fairly deep dish, pour over the honey and vinegar mixture, season with pepper, cover with plastic wrap and leave to marinate for at least 8 hours.

Broiled bell peppers

Cut the bell peppers in half lengthwise and place them under a very hot broiler until the skin blisters. Put them in a plastic bag and seal it so that the peppers sweat—they'll be easier to peel. Alternatively, you could buy some precooked broiled bell peppers.

Another method is to broil them directly over the gas flame (as in the photo on the previous page), but take care not to burn your fingers.

Roast tomatoes

Serves 4–6
Preparation time: 5 minutes
Cooking time: 2½ hours

About 10 small, very ripe Italian tomatoes
3 tablespoons olive oil
1 tablespoon superfine sugar

Cut the tomatoes in half and lay the halves side by side in a gratin dish, cut side up. Mix the olive oil and the sugar together. Pour over the tomatoes. Cook in the oven at 300° F for about 2½ hours. The caramel that forms at the bottom of the dish is delicious!

If you're using small cherry tomatoes, leave them on the vine for a more elegant presentation.

Small roast tomatoes could be used to make a tomato clafouti (see page 124), while larger ones could be whizzed in a blender to make a rich, tasty soup to be served hot or cold.

Red cabbage and apples braised in balsamic vinegar

A marvelous accompaniment to roast duck (page 103) and game.

Serves 6–8
Preparation time: 15 minutes
Cooking time: 1½ hours

1 large pan

2 onions, finely chopped
½ cup duck fat
3 cooking apples, peeled and chopped
⅔ cup red wine
⅓ cup apple juice
¾ cup balsamic vinegar
1 tablespoon brown sugar
about 10 juniper berries, crushed
2 lb 4 oz red cabbage, shredded
salt and pepper

Place all the ingredients, except for the cabbage, in the pan. Bring to a boil, then add the cabbage. Return to a boil, then reduce the heat and simmer for about 1½ hours. If the cabbage dries out too much, add some more apple juice.
Season and serve.

Ratatouille

Serves 8
Preparation time: 25 minutes
Cooking time: 1 hour

1 large, deep skillet

1 lb zucchini, sliced
1 lb eggplants, cubed
1 lb onions, thinly sliced
1 lb green bell peppers, seeded and sliced
5 cloves garlic, crushed
1 lb 12 oz tomatoes, peeled, seeded, and cut in half (or 2 large cans tomatoes)
salt and black pepper
thyme, basil, and parsley
⅔ cup olive oil

Heat half the oil in the skillet. Sauté the zucchini lightly. Add the eggplant and continue to cook. Remove the vegetables and set aside.
Put the rest of the oil in the skillet with the onions and fry them until they are very soft. Add the bell peppers and garlic. Turn up the heat and cook for a few minutes longer. Add the tomatoes and cook for a further 10 minutes.
Add the eggplant and zucchini, mix everything together thoroughly, season, add some thyme and simmer uncovered for 40 to 45 minutes.
Just before serving, shred the basil leaves and add them to the ratatouille with the chopped parsley. Delicious eaten hot or cold, and especially delicious when reheated.

Bell pepper salsa (Piperade)

A Basque specialty

Serves 8
Preparation time: 20 minutes
Cooking time: 1 hour

1 large, deep skillet

7–8 tablespoons olive oil
3 onions, finely chopped
2 lb 4 oz red and green bell peppers, seeded and sliced
2 cloves garlic, finely chopped
1 tablespoon sugar
2 lb 4 oz tomatoes, peeled, seeded and quartered
1 bouquet garni
salt and black pepper

Heat 3 tablespoons of oil and sauté the onions very gently without allowing them to brown. Add all the other ingredients. Season with salt and pepper and simmer for 40 to 45 minutes.
If you're using preserved peppers, add them 15 minutes before the end of the cooking time.
Some raw ham and beaten eggs cooked in the vegetables for 5 minutes will turn this side dish into a meal in its own right.

Tian of eggplant, tomatoes, and onions

Serves 4–6
Preparation time: 20 minutes
Cooking time: 2 hours

1 earthenware dish with a lid

3 tablespoons olive oil
4 eggplants, cubed
2 onions, finely chopped
4 tomatoes, peeled and seeded
3 cloves garlic, crushed
salt and pepper
thyme, bay leaf and parsley

Preheat the oven to 350° F.
Heat the oil in a large casserole dish and brown the eggplants and onions. Add the tomatoes, garlic, salt, pepper, and chopped herbs.
Put everything in an earthenware, ovenproof dish with a lid. Cover and cook in the oven for 2 hours, stirring gently once or twice.

Mashed potatoes—the sequel

IN MY PREVIOUS BOOK *Cooking with Friends*, the page on mashed potatoes met with great success. By popular demand, here are a few new variations to add to your repertoire.

Stewed onions with broiled pine nuts

Brown some onions with a little olive oil and butter heated in a skillet. Reduce the heat, add a little sugar, and stew for 15 minutes. Toast the pine nuts in a pan or another skillet.
Place a little pile of onions on each portion of mash and sprinkle with pine nuts.

Horseradish

Add 2 teaspoons of horseradish relish to each portion of potatoes. Delicious with beef or pan-fried tuna or swordfish.

Peas with bacon

Cook some frozen peas in boiling salted water for a little longer than indicated on the packet. Brown some cubes of bacon or pancetta and mix them with the peas, mashed with butter, a little lemon juice, and light cream. Delicious with roast belly of pork (page 34).

Spiced sweet potatoes

Make a mash with equal quantities of regular and sweet potatoes. Add some spices, perhaps nutmeg, cinnamon, and ground ginger depending on your taste. Excellent with game.

Carrots and parsnips

Mashed and mixed with carrots, parsnips make an excellent accompaniment for slow-cooked dishes.

EASY DESSERTS

Figs stewed in port

Serves 6–8
Preparation time: 2 minutes
Cooking time: 25 minutes

1 pan

½ cup water
4 tablespoons sugar
1 cup port
juice and rind of 1 lemon
1 vanilla bean, split lengthwise
1 bay leaf
8 very ripe figs

Make a syrup by putting all the ingredients, except for the figs, in a saucepan. Bring to a boil slowly, then reduce for 10 to 15 minutes.
Quarter the figs, add them to the syrup and stew very gently for a further 10 minutes.
Leave to cool completely before serving.

Cherries in kirsch

Unless you want hands worthy of a mechanic, equip yourself with gloves and a cherry pitter!

Serves 6
Preparation time: 30 minutes
Cooking time: 10 minutes
Cooling time: 2–3 hours

1 pan

1 lb 12 oz pitted cherries
½ cup sugar
2 tablespoons water
2 tablespoons kirsch liqueur

Put the cherries, water, and sugar in a saucepan. Bring to a boil and stew for 5 to 10 minutes. Drain and put the juice to one side.
Mix half of the cherries with the juice and then add the kirsch and the rest of the cherries. Stir well and leave to cool in the refrigerator for 2 to 3 hours.

Baked tamarillos

The tamarillo, a South American fruit also known as a tree tomato, has something of the tomato, plum, and nectarine about it. They used to be one of those fruits that perplexed me when I saw them on the exotic fruit stalls, because I didn't know exactly what to do with them.

I tasted them for the first time at the *Sugar Club* in London, a real "fusion" restaurant. Now I never miss an opportunity to cook them. However, such opportunities are rare…
After all, the exotic fruits that end up in supermarkets are not always perfect. They are often incorrectly stored and either unripe or overripe, making it difficult to select good ones. When choosing your tamarillos, think of ripe nectarines. That's what they're supposed to resemble.

Serves 4
Preparation time: 5 minutes
Cooking time: 45 minutes

1 gratin dish

2 tamarillos
4 tablespoons sugar
3 oz (¾ stick) butter

Preheat the oven to 300° F.
Cut the tamarillos in half and put some sugar and butter on each half.
Bake for 45 minutes.
Serve lukewarm with mascarpone or vanilla ice cream.

Baked fruit salad with butter

Serves 6
Preparation time: 3 minutes
Cooking time: 15 minutes

1 gratin dish

6 figs
6 peaches
6 plums
2 handfuls red grapes
2 tablespoons brown sugar
2 oz (½ stick) butter

Preheat the oven to 400° F.
Place the fruit and sugar in the dish, dot with butter, and bake for 15 minutes.
Serve with good vanilla ice cream or stirred custard flavored with bay leaves.

TIP • Follow the same recipe using sliced pineapple instead of the figs, grapes, and pit fruit.

Baked quinces with vanilla

A fairly rare fruit and therefore a truly seasonal one. There's no photo because the ones on my kind neighbor's tree were still very small. But that won't stop him giving me some this year…

Serves 6
Preparation time: 5 minutes
Cooking time: 2 hours

1 heavy-based dish with a lid
1¼ cups red wine
⅔ cup sugar
1 vanilla bean, split lengthwise
6 small or 3 large quinces, peeled and cut in half

Preheat the oven 300° F.
Place the wine, sugar, vanilla bean, and ¾ cup water in the dish. Heat gently until the sugar is totally dissolved. Place the quinces in the liquid, cover, and bake for 1 hour.
Uncover and continue to cook for another 1 to 1½ hours.
Serve with vanilla ice cream, or mascarpone and the cooking liquid.

Peaches stewed in white wine

A recipe derived from one of Raymond Blanc's: it's done the rounds of my sisters-in-law and friends. One of my favorite summer desserts: elegant, delicious, and simple.

Serves 6
Preparation time: 10 minutes
Cooking time: 25 minutes

1 pan

1 orange
1 lemon
6 nice ripe peaches
2 cups white wine
1¼ cups water
½ cup sugar
2 vanilla beans
2 cloves

Thinly slice the orange and lemon. Lay the peaches side by side in a pan. Pour on the wine and water and add the sugar. Split the vanilla beans lengthwise and add them to the pan, together with the cloves. Place the orange and lemon slices on top.
Bring to a boil and simmer very gently for 20 to 25 minutes.
Leave the peaches to cool in the syrup.
When they're cold, take off the skins and place them in the serving dish with the vanilla beans and the orange and lemon slices.
Pour the cold syrup over them and leave to stand for at least 8 hours, or overnight if possible.

Melon with lime and ginger

Melon gently simmered in this very aromatic syrup should be left untouched in the refrigerator for at least 2 to 3 hours.

Serves 6
Preparation time: 15 minutes
Chilling time: at least 2 hours

1 pan
1¾ cups water
1 cup dry white wine
1 cup superfine sugar
juice of 2 limes
rind of 1 lime
1 piece fresh ginger the size of your thumb, finely chopped
1 lb fresh or frozen melon balls

Place all the ingredients, except for the melon, in a pan and heat gently until the sugar is totally dissolved. Add the melon and bring to a boil, then simmer over a gentle heat for 3 minutes. Remove from the heat, take out the melon, and set it aside.
Reduce the syrup for about 10 minutes until it is thicker and more concentrated.
Leave to cool for a few minutes and then add the melon balls. When it has completely cooled, put everything in the refrigerator for at least 2 hours, ideally overnight.
Serve with little Chinese sesame and honey cakes, available from shops specializing in oriental food items.

Fruit compotes
Apples in caramel

Serves 4–6
Preparation time: 15 minutes
Cooking time: 25 minutes

1 regular pan
1 small, heavy-based pan

3 lb 5 oz apples
4–5 tablespoons sugar

For the caramel
½ cup sugar
2 oz (½ stick) butter

Peel, core, and slice the apples. Put them in a pan with the sugar and a little water. Cook gently for about 15 minutes and then purée them with a potato masher.
Make the caramel by heating the sugar in a heavy-based pan. When a nice golden caramel has formed, add the butter and stir vigorously. Return to the heat and, if necessary, add a little light cream in order to disperse any lumps.

Variations
Pear, peach, vanilla

Cook for a slightly shorter time, using less sugar and adding a split vanilla bean.

Rhubarb, ginger, strawberry

Add a piece of ginger to the rhubarb.
Top and tail the strawberries and add them to the cooked rhubarb.
They will release their juices as they cook.

Orange salad with olive oil

Serves 4
Preparation time: 10 minutes

4 oranges
a few drops olive oil

Peel the oranges and slice them, retaining the juice.
Add a few drops of very good olive oil and serve well chilled.

Ricotta with vanilla and maple syrup

Serves 4
Preparation time: 3 minutes
1 vanilla bean
4–6 tablespoons maple syrup
1¼ cups ricotta, drained

Split the vanilla bean and scrape out the seeds. Mix them with the maple syrup.
Break up the ricotta and pour the syrup over it. Leave to marinate for 1 hour in a cool place and serve.

Rice pudding – great stuff!

Some people used to find it very difficult to finish a plate of rice pudding. Here's a revised, deluxe version that should help to dispel memories of the gloop grandma used to serve up.

Serves 6
Preparation time: 5 minutes
Cooking time: 25 minutes

1 pan

½ cup sugar
3 cups milk
1 cup light cream
1 vanilla bean, split lengthwise
2½ cups round-grain rice (Arborio) or pudding rice

To serve
2–3 tablespoons brown sugar
or sweetened chestnut purée
or caramel fruit compote (page 154)
or 2–3 tablespoons mascarpone
(when the rice is still hot or lukewarm)

Add the sugar to the milk and cream. Bring to a boil. Add the split vanilla bean and the rice and cook for about 20 minutes, stirring continuously. All the milk must be absorbed and the rice so soft it melts in the mouth.
Add some milk if the mixture becomes too sticky. Serve hot, lukewarm, or cold with one or more of the suggested accompaniments.

WARNING • The following recipe contains raw eggs. It is not advisable to serve this dish to very young children, pregnant women, elderly people or anyone weakened by serious illness. Be sure that the eggs are as fresh as possible. If in any doubt, consult your doctor.

Chilled coffee gateau

A little recipe of my mother's that requires no cooking, just good construction skills…

Serves 6–8
Preparation time: 20 minutes
Refrigeration time: overnight

1 cake pan (a flexible silicone mold would be ideal here)
1 electric mixer

1 tablespoon rum or amaretto
¾ cup very strong black coffee
4½ oz (1 stick + 1 tablespoon) unsalted butter, softened
½ cup sugar
2 egg yolks
2 packets ladyfingers
2 tablespoons chopped walnuts or crushed amaretto biscuits

Line the cake pan with plastic wrap if you don't have a flexible silicone mold.
Mix the rum and the coffee and leave until completely cool.
Cream the butter and sugar until the mixture turns pale and frothy.
Add the egg yolks and beat well so that everything is thoroughly mixed together.
Completely cover the bottom of the cake pan with one third of the ladyfingers. Pour on one third of the coffee. Spread half of the butter cream over the ladyfingers. Repeat once and then cover with the last third of the ladyfingers. Pour on the rest of the coffee.
Cover the cake with a plate and weight it down with cans of tomatoes, cartons of milk, etc. Leave it to chill in the refrigerator overnight.
Turn the cake out of the cake pan and decorate it with chopped walnuts or crushed amaretto biscuits.

THIS IS THE DESSERT EVERYBODY MAKES FUN OF… before eating and enjoying it! It's true that dreadful versions of the traditional sherry trifle, based on instant custard and Jello, did once exist. At the time, it was the British equivalent of the chocolate mousse out of a packet dished up in self-service restaurants across continental Europe.

With today's renewed interest in culinary traditions, I'm delighted to say that we are witnessing the rebirth of magnificent trifles. If I were you, I'd give this old-fashioned name to any dessert consisting of alternate layers of fruit, cream, egg custard, and ladyfingers. Here's the method. The rest is up to you.

The cream

Use fresh whipping cream, possibly mixed with some mascarpone for a smoother, more luxurious texture, whipped together using an electric mixer. You could also add some egg yolks to give it the richness of tiramisu, in which case you could dispense with the layer of egg custard.

For a large trifle, take 1¼ cups light cream, a small container of mascarpone, 2 to 3 tablespoons of sugar, and 3 egg yolks. The layer of cream could be flavored with chocolate (milk, white, or dark), coffee, or various liqueurs (e.g. Baileys, rum, amaretto, Grand Marnier).

The fruit

The trifles of my childhood were made with strawberry or raspberry Jello with pieces of tinned pear, pineapple, and cherries in it.
It's easier—and much tastier—to use red fruits when they're in season (raspberries for preference, because of their delicious juice) or stewed acidic fruit, such as apricots, rhubarb, or plums.

The ladyfingers

As an alternative to ordinary ladyfingers, you could use Italian macaroons (amaretti).
A layer of granola mix would also be delicious and make for a crunchier texture.

The egg custard

Making it is tricky, but once you've mastered the technique, you'll be able to give the whole world a treat. My friend Armelle's version is so good she serves it on its own as a dessert in stemmed glasses! Here's a fairly rich version intended to blend with the layers of fruit and cream in your trifle.

Preparation time: 10 minutes
Cooking time: 10 minutes

1 or 2 vanilla beans
1 cup milk
1 cup light cream
6 egg yolks
⅔ cup sugar

Split the vanilla beans and put them in a pan with the milk and cream. Bring to a boil. Meanwhile, whisk the egg yolks with the sugar until the mixture turns pale and doubles in volume. Pour the milk and cream mixture over the eggs, stirring vigorously. Pour everything back into the pan and heat, stirring continuously with a wooden spoon. Cook until the mixture thickens, being very careful not to let it boil.
When it thickens, remove it from the heat immediately. Since it continues to cook even when removed from the heat and the bottom of the pan cooks quicker than the rest, I always pour the egg custard into another container, chilled if possible, stopping before I reach the bottom of the pan. If, by any chance, you spot any lumps, beat vigorously with the wooden spoon until they disappear.

Ladyfingers

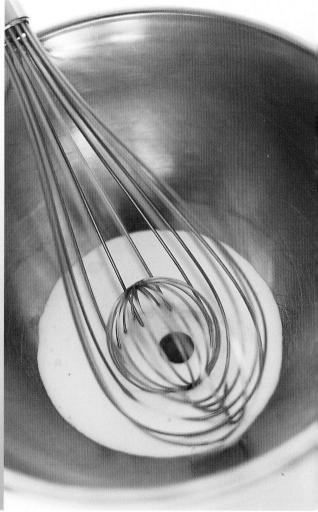

Egg custard

Assembling a trifle

Try the following combinations

Cream flavored with white chocolate, rhubarb, and ladyfingers

Raspberries with honey
cream flavored with whisky, layers of granola
(right)

Amaretti biscuits soaked in coffee, tiramisu cream

Ladyfingers soaked in sherry, raspberries, whipped cream, and egg custard

Ladyfingers, stewed apricots with vanilla, whipped cream

Amaretti biscuits soaked in rum, a layer of melted chocolate, egg custard, and whipped cream

Apple compote with orange rind, cream flavored with Grand Marnier, ladyfingers (left)

The method

Put together alternate layers of ladyfingers soaked in alcohol, coffee, or fruit juice, and fruit, cream and egg custard. Leave overnight in the refrigerator if possible to give the flavors and textures time to mingle.

Experiment with serving dishes. Individual trifles made in glasses or small bowls are pretty (and fashionable). For a more spectacular effect and a shorter preparation time, use a large bowl.

Even if, like me, you're not terribly dexterous and your layers are a little uneven and jumbled up, the result will still be attractive and delicious.

SAVING FOR A RAINY DAY

How can you feel beneficent, protective and close to nature all at the same time? By making jams, chutneys and preserves. It's amazingly therapeutic, I promise you—second only to eating chocolate—and a very effective way to offset life's trials and tribulations.

It's incredible how quickly one takes to playing Mrs Ingalls in *The Little House on the Prairie*, willing to do anything to protect one's little family throughout the long winter against marauding bears and snowstorms.

I'm not going to force you to struggle with sterilization techniques nor to prepare tons of green beans. Deep-frozen products will do nicely, thankfully. These recipes are intended rather as easy side dishes that will liven up your breakfasts and plates of cold cuts, or make excellent desserts.

Bottled fruit

This fruit preserved in alcohol takes two months to develop its full flavor.

You will need a large sterilized jar and a good colorless spirit, vodka or marc de Bourgogne, for example. (See TIP, page 48 for method of sterilizing jars.)

With the passing seasons, carefully place very ripe but unblemished fruit in the jar, adding 4½ cups of sugar for each 2 lb 4 oz of fruit, pouring in more alcohol with each new batch of fruit in order to keep everything covered. Do not stir.

Begin with strawberries, raspberries, and cherries (stoned or whole). Then add quartered apricots, slices of white and yellow peaches, and chopped plums and pears. Put some grape seeds in as well and resist temptation for two or three months. Serve as an after-dinner liqueur in small glasses.

Dried and crystallized fruit in muscatel wine

This is a "trick of the trade" rather than a recipe, a confidence imparted by the man who sells me my dried and crystallized fruit.

Put the fruit (here, apricots, crystallized clementines, dates, muscatels, and dried peaches and pineapple) in a clean, sterilized jar together with some hazelnuts, almonds, and walnuts and fill the jar with muscatel wine. Screw the lid down tightly and store for 2 or 3 months in a closet or in the cellar.

(See TIP, page 48 for method of sterilizing jars.)

Prunes in Armagnac

Something delicious to keep at the back of the larder for impromptu dinners. Absolutely divine with vanilla ice cream and hot chocolate sauce. Also very useful when one is invited out to dinner and asked to bring the dessert.

Preparation time: 5 minutes
Cooking time: 5 minutes
Waiting time: 2 weeks

1 pan
3 sterilized jelly jars with screw lids (see Tip page 48 for sterilization method)

1 cup water
½ cup sugar
1 lb prunes
3 cloves
3 small pieces cinnamon stick
rind of 1 orange and ½ lemon
¾ cup Armagnac

Make a syrup by boiling the water and sugar for 5 minutes.
Place the prunes with the spices and orange and lemon rind in the sterilized jars.
Leave the syrup to cool and then divide it up among the three jars. Fill to the top with Armagnac, screw down the lids firmly and keep in a cool, dark place for two weeks before sampling.

Orange marmalade

Preparation time: 30 minutes
Cooking time: 1 hour
Soaking time: overnight

1 large casserole dish or preserving pan
1 bowl
1 mixing bowl
about 6 jelly jars

3 lb 4 oz Seville oranges
5 lb 8 oz / 12 cups sugar

First sterilize the jars (see TIP, page 48).
Peel the oranges. Cut the peel into strips and chop the flesh, taking care to save the seeds. Put the seeds into the bowl and the rest of the oranges into the mixing bowl.
Bring 6 pints/15 cups water to a boil. Pour 2½ cups boiling water over the seeds and the rest into the mixing bowl.
Cover the bowl and the mixing bowl and leave to stand overnight.
Next day, the seeds will be covered with a jelly known as pectin. In order to collect it, put the seeds in a strainer and rinse them carefully over the mixing bowl with the water used to soak the peel and the seeds.
Place the contents of the mixing bowl into a large casserole dish or preserving pan and simmer until the peel turns very soft. Remove from the heat, add the sugar, and stir until it has completely dissolved.
Bring to a boil again and cook vigorously for a further 15 minutes. When the marmalade is cooked, skim the surface, leave to stand for 15 minutes, and then stir well in order to distribute the peel.
Pour into jars and seal tightly.

Preserved apricots with vanilla

Makes about 10 jars
Preparation time: 30 minutes
Cooking time: 5 minutes
Maceration time: 10–12 hours

6 lb 8 oz apricots
3 vanilla beans
5 lb 8 oz/12 cups sugar
juice of half a lemon

First sterilize the jars (see TIP, page 48).
Quickly wash the apricots. Remove the pits and chop the flesh. Cut the vanilla beans in two and cut each half into 12 pieces. Place the apricots in a preserving pan or large pan and add the sugar, lemon juice, and vanilla. Leave to macerate until the sugar is completely dissolved. Cook over a high heat for 5 minutes, stirring constantly.
Put into jars, adding a piece of vanilla bean to each jar.

TIP • Make sure your vanilla beans are large, shiny, and soft. Delicatessens usually sell good ones. Vanilla beans keep very well in a dry place. Everyone will advise you to keep them in sugar, but you may end up just with flavored sugar and dried-out vanilla beans. I prefer to keep them fresh in a tightly sealed jar in a cool closet.

Lime curd

Makes 2 small jars
Preparation time: 15 minutes
Cooking time: 20 minutes

rind and juice of 3 limes
4 eggs
¾ cup sugar
4 oz (1 stick) butter

Carefully grate the rind and then squeeze the
limes to extract the juice. Mix together the juice
and eggs in a bowl and add the sugar. Cut the
butter into small pieces, add to the bowl and then
place the bowl on top of a pan of boiling water
(or use a double boiler). Stir constantly for
20 minutes until the mixture thickens. Leave to
cool, stirring from time to time.

TIP • Lime curd is the perfect filling for a tart.
Bake a pastry case using pie crust pastry (see
page 90). Leave to cool and fill with the lime
curd.

Caramelized milk
(the real thing)

Makes 6–7 jars
Cooking time: 2 1/2 hours

1 large, heavy-based pan

7 pints/14 cups milk
4 lb 8 oz/9 cups superfine sugar
4 vanilla beans, split lengthwise

First sterilize the jars (see TIP, page 48).
Pour the milk into the pan with the sugar and
bring gently to a boil. Add the vanilla beans
Simmer over a gentle heat for 2½ hours until the
milk has thickened and taken on a pretty caramel
color.
Pour into jars and close the lids tightly. The
caramelized milk will keep for up to 3 months.

Caramelized milk
(for cheats)

Cooking time: 3 hours
1 can sweetened condensed milk

Make a tiny hole in the top of the can. Put it in a
pan, then fill pan with water to below the top of
the can (see photo opposite). Bring to a boil, turn
down the heat, and boil gently for 3 hours. The
milk will caramelize. Leave to cool before serving.

Red onion jam

Serves 6–8
Preparation time: 10 minutes
Cooking time: 1 hour

1 skillet

1¼ cups golden raisins
4–5 tablespoons olive oil
2 lb 4 oz red onions, finely sliced
⅔ cup sugar
1 cup red wine
3 tablespoons balsamic vinegar
3 tablespoons crème de cassis (or port)

Plump up the golden raisins in warm water for about 30 minutes. Drain and set aside.
Heat the oil in the skillet. Fry the onions for 10 to 15 minutes over a moderate heat.
Add the sugar, reduce the heat, and cook for a further 10 minutes until the onions are very soft and caramelized.
Add the golden raisins, wine, vinegar, and crème de cassis (or port). Cook for 25 to 30 minutes until all the liquid has been absorbed and the jam is nice and thick. Season and leave to cool completely.
This jam will keep 2 to 3 weeks in a sealed container stored in a cool, dry, dark place.

Quick tomato and apple chutney

Makes about 2 lb 4 oz
Preparation time: 10 minutes
Cooking time: 25 minutes

1 deep skillet
1 small pan

1 tablespoon olive oil
1 onion, finely chopped
½ teaspoon mixed-spice powder
1 cooking apple, peeled and chopped
2 tablespoons white wine vinegar
1 tablespoon soft brown sugar
2 cups canned chopped tomatoes
1 tablespoon tomato paste
Worcestershire sauce
salt and pepper

First sterilize the jar (see TIP, page 48).
Heat the oil in a skillet and brown the onion for a few minutes. Add the mixed-spice powder and the apple and cook for a little longer. Pour on the vinegar, add the sugar, bring to a boil, and simmer until there is virtually no liquid left.
Add the tomatoes and the tomato paste and cook for a few more minutes.
Season with the Worcestershire sauce, salt, and pepper.
Put the chutney through a strainer.
Put the liquid in a pan and reduce it to obtain a thicker syrup.
Stir the syrup into the chutney and put into a sealed container. It will keep for a week in the refrigerator.

Sweet and sour cherries

Preparation time: 20 minutes

4–5 jars with lids
1 pan

4 lb 8 oz very ripe cherries (avoid blemished fruit)
4–5 tablespoons sugar
6 cups white wine vinegar
6–8 black peppercorns
2 cloves
1 bay leaf
salt

First sterilize the jars (see TIP, page 48).
Leave just ¼ inch of stalk on the cherries, then wash and dry them thoroughly. Place them in the jars and sprinkle with the sugar.
Bring 4 cups of vinegar to a boil with the peppercorns, cloves, bay leaf, and a little salt. Boil for about 5 minutes. Leave to cool, then pour over the cherries and leave to marinate for 24 hours.
The next day, drain the marinade off the cherries, add the rest of the vinegar to it, and boil for 10 minutes. Fill the jars with cherries, put over the vinegar, and tap to release any air bubbles. Put the lids on the jars.
Leave for a month before sampling.

Fig and golden raisin chutney with jasmine tea

Preparation time: 10 minutes
Cooking time: 10 minutes
Cooling time: 2 hours

1 pan

1 teaspoon jasmine tea, or teabag
rind and juice of 1 orange and ½ lemon or lime
3 tablespoons sugar
2 black peppercorns
1 clove
6 very ripe figs
2 tablespoons golden raisins

Make a cup of very strong tea, leaving to infuse for 10–15 minutes. Add the orange and lemon rind, sugar, peppercorns, and clove. Bring to a boil and cook until the liquid has reduced to half its volume.
Cut the figs into 1 inch pieces and place them in a mixing bowl with the golden raisins.
Pour the tea syrup over the fruit through a tea strainer.
Put everything in the pan and simmer gently for a few minutes.
Leave to cool and serve with cold cuts.

USEFUL THINGS

My utensils

(clockwise from top, left)

Roasting rack
Very useful for browning the underside of joints of roast meat and for collecting and draining off the fat that drips into the roasting pan.

Earthenware terrine
Ideal for terrines of meat and vegetable tians.

Roasting pan
Very simple and widely available in department stores and supermarkets, they come in all sizes.

Potato masher
Essential for making successful mashes.

Pie funnel
Designed to hold the pie crust together and let out the air that accumulates underneath it in tarts and pies.

A good, heavy-based, nonstick pan or casserole dish
It makes life so much easier!

Measuring pitcher
Personally, for small quantities, I also use a baby's feeding bottle. A little disconcerting all the same when it comes to measuring out brandy…

My beloved little enamel casserole
Sold in department stores and supermarkets as well as in hardware stores. There's no need to go to one of the trendy cook shops that are often so intimidating.

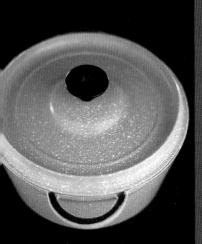

Roasting rack

Terrine

Roasting tin

Masher

Pie funnel

Casserole

I HAVE A BIG PROBLEM WITH BARBECUES. I know that they're supposed to be the ultimate in informal meals with family and friends, but I don't like them unless they're at other people's houses. There's one simple fact about barbecues: either the food's burnt to a cinder or you get to eat lunch at "tea-time." In any case, everything tastes of firelighters. What's more, my husband turns into Neanderthal man, willing to do anything to protect his hearth from other members of the tribe. I feel ousted from my role as mother-provider and the atmosphere always ends up becoming a little frosty, despite its being 80° F in the shade. So here are a few ideas for marinades I'd be delighted to try the next time you invite me to your home!

For tuna or swordfish steaks

Blend together some melted butter, broiled bell peppers, lemon juice, salt, and pepper. Coat the fish with this sauce before cooking it. It imparts a deliciously crisp texture, crunchy even, since the steaks will have fallen into the sand a couple of times while being cooked…

For lamb chops

Blend some yogurt with cloves of garlic and goat's cheese. Add some finely chopped mint and dill and some olive oil.
Coat the chops with this mixture and cook for 3 to 4 minutes on each side. (Actually, between you and me, you should probably allow 20 to 25 minutes because you will have forgotten to keep the coals hot!)

For chicken breasts

1 tablespoon mango chutney
1 tablespoon olive oil
1 tablespoon ketchup
1 tablespoon Worcestershire sauce
1 tablespoon mustard
2 tablespoons brown sugar
3 tablespoons orange juice
salt and pepper
(1 bottle of shower gel to get rid of the smell of smoke before you go to bed!)

Mix all the ingredients together (except the shower gel), pour over the chicken and leave to marinate for 30 minutes before chargrilling for 4 to 5 minutes on each side.

Marinated sardines

This is perhaps the only barbecue recipe I would make with a smile on my lips, since marinated sardines taste as good raw as cooked. Leave them to marinate for about 2 hours in a mixture of olive oil, lemon and lime juice and peel, salt, and pepper. Then it's up to you whether to barbecue them, at your own risk of course. It would be a shame to spoil them, though.

Most of these stocks are essential for making sauces, soups, broths, meat glazes, etc. They will keep for 3 or 4 days in the refrigerator or you can freeze them in small quantities and keep them for several months in the freezer, to serve your needs.

Chicken stock

Makes about 6 cups
Preparation time: 10 minutes
Cooking time: 2 hours

1 large pan
1 strainer

1 chicken, about 3 lb 5 oz in weight
1 onion, stuck with cloves
2 leeks, cut into rounds
2 stalks celery with leaves, chopped
1 bay leaf
5 pints/12 cups cold water
5 black peppercorns

Place all the ingredients in a large pan. Bring to a boil gently and turn down the heat immediately. Cover and simmer for about 1½ hours, skimming if necessary. Leave to cool for 30 minutes, remove the fat from the surface with kitchen towel, then put the stock through a strainer.
Throw away any solids left in the strainer.

Beef stock

Makes about 6 cups
Preparation time: 10 minutes
Cooking time: 2 hours

1 large saucepan
1 strainer

2lb 4 oz raw or cooked beef bones and meat
2 carrots, cut into rounds
1 onion, peeled and stuck with 2 cloves
2 stalks celery, roughly chopped
2 leeks, cut into rounds
1 bouquet garni
5 pints/12 cups cold water
5 black peppercorns

Place all the ingredients in a large pan. Bring to a boil gently and turn down the heat. Cover and simmer for about 1½ hours, skimming if necessary. Leave to cool, remove the fat from the surface with kitchen towel, then put the stock through a strainer.
Throw away any solids left in the strainer.

Fish stock

Makes about 4 cups
Preparation time: 10 minutes
Cooking time: 25 minutes

1 large pan
1 strainer

2 lb 4 oz fish bones
3 shallots, finely chopped
2 tablespoons butter
8 oz white mushrooms, chopped
2 carrots, cut into rounds
1 leek, cut into rounds
6 cups cold water
1 bouquet garni

Place all the ingredients in a large pan and bring to a boil slowly. Simmer for 25 minutes, skimming the surface from time to time. Leave to cool and then put through a strainer. Discard all but the liquid.

Be careful: fish bones give a bitter taste if they cook for too long.

Vegetable stock

Makes about 6 cups
Preparation time: 10 minutes
Cooking time: 1–2 hours

1 large pan
1 strainer

2 tablespoons butter
1 lb onions, minced
1 lb carrots, cut into rounds
4 stalks celery with leaves, coarsely chopped
8 cups cold water
10 white peppercorns
1 bouquet garni

Melt the butter in a large pan. Cook the vegetables gently until they turn pale yellow. Do not under any circumstances allow them to turn golden or brown, because it will spoil the taste of the stock.
Add the water, the peppercorns and the bouquet garni.
Bring to a boil slowly. Reduce the heat, skim the surface if necessary, then half-cover the pan and simmer very gently for 1–2 hours.
Put the stock through a fine strainer and leave to cool. Discard the solids.

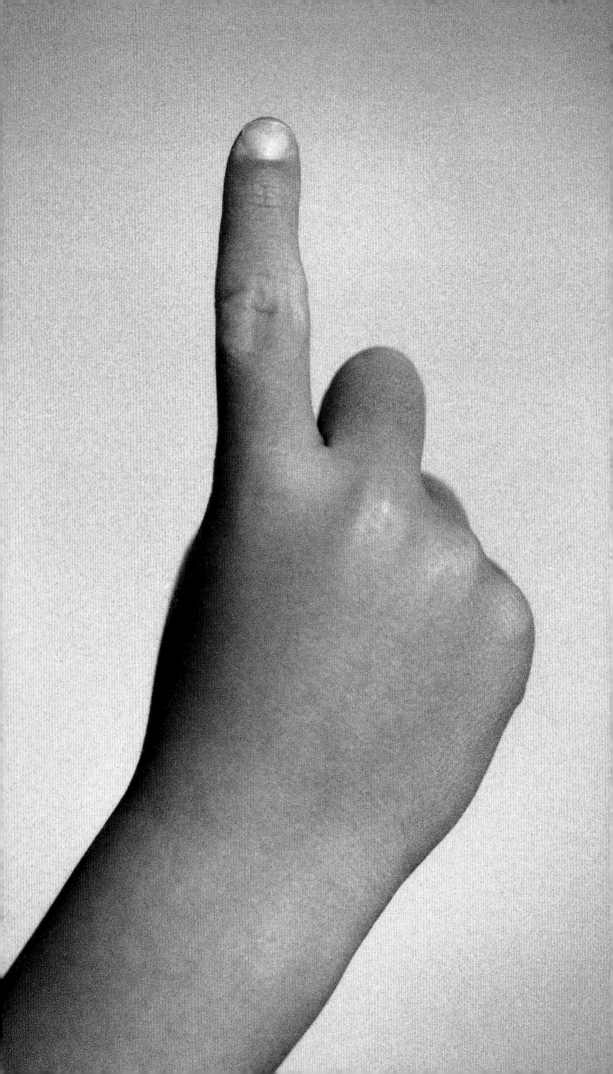

INDEX

Index

In memory of my father, Herbie Stevens, who cooked a mean pot-roast

Acknowledgments

My thanks to:
- the Marabout dream team and Sylvain
- the Maison La Cornue, and in particular Pauline de Vilmorin
- Monsieur and Madame Boudinet, tripe butchers at Saint-Germain-en-Laye market
- the Deseines of the Moulin de Brasseuil, for the photo session
- the Maison Frichot in Boinville, official supplier of potatoes
- Jacqueline for the bottling evening
- the village brainstormers
- my girlfriends and their glamor for their recipes
- and to Thierry, who always lights my fire.

Shopping and table decoration:

Staub, cast-iron plate, p. 13, p. 51; square cast-iron plate, p. 143.
La Cornue, large casserole dish, p. 71.

Farm and forest figurines:

Schleich (on sale in some department stores and toyshops).

Text and recipes © Trish Deseine
Photography © Sylvain Thomas

French edition: © Marabout (Hachette Livre), 2002
English edition: © Hachette Illustrated 2004

This edition published by Hachette Illustrated UK, Octopus Publishing Group Ltd.,
2-4 Heron Quay, London E14 4JP

English text produced by Book Production Consultants plc, Cambridge
English translation © Octopus 2004

ISBN 1-84430-072-2
Printed in Singapore by Tien Wah Press